The Documentation

A Pocket Guide
Custom Edition

Michael Pringle

John Gonzales

Taken from:
The APA Style of Documentation: A Pocket Guide
by Michael Pringle and John Gonzales

Learning Solutions

New York   Boston   San Francisco
London   Toronto   Sydney   Tokyo   Singapore   Madrid
Mexico City   Munich   Paris   Cape Town   Hong Kong   Montreal

Taken from:

The APA Style of Documentation: A Pocket Guide
by Michael Pringle and John Gonzales
Copyright © 2010 by Pearson Education, Inc.
Published by Prentice Hall
Upper Saddle River, NJ 07458

This special edition published in cooperation with Pearson Learning Solutions.

Pearson Learning Solutions, 501 Boylston Street, Suite 900, Boston, MA 02116
A Pearson Education Company
www.pearsoned.com

Printed in the United States of America

2 3 4 5 6 7 8 9 10   V313   15 14 13 12 11

000200010270652958

ST

ISBN 10: 0-558-94818-9
ISBN 13: 978-0-558-94818-4

Contents

Preface

The APA Style of Documentation: A Pocket Guide demonstrates the fundamentals of documentation for collegiate writing. It also offers a discussion of academic honesty, a sample student essay, and a helpful section on finding, evaluating, and integrating sources. It should prove sufficient for most undergraduate needs, and it will remain a useful reference even for graduate students.

This guide is intended as a handy reference for citing accurately in the APA format. It concentrates on the types of sources students are most likely to use, but while it covers a broad range, it is not comprehensive. The definitive guide remains the *Publication Manual of the American Psychological Association,* 6th ed. (2010). More advanced students considering submitting an essay for publication in a scholarly journal should refer to the APA *Publication Manual.*

This book has greatly benefited by attention from the editor and copyeditors. We would like to thank them for their expert assistance. We are also indebted to the reviewers who helped improve the guide by providing thoughtful and astute commentary. They are: James Allen, College of DuPage; Anne Balay, Indiana University Northwest; Rochelle Becker-Bernstein, St. Johns River Community College; A. Boumarate, Valencia Community College; Mark Coley, Tarrant County College; Mark Crane, Utah Valley University; Christopher J. L. Cunningham, University of Tennessee at Chattanooga; Jason Denman, Utica College; Bonnie Devet, College of Charleston; Michael W. Donaghe, Eastern New Mexico University; David B. Downing, Indiana University of Pennsylvania; Beverly D. Fatherree, Hinds Community College; Karen Gardiner, University of Alabama; Michael Hricik, Westmoreland County Community College; Holly Hunt, Metropolitan State College of Denver; JoAnne James, Pitt Community College; Cynthia Kuhn, Metro State; Terry Mathias, Southeastern Illinois College; Susan Miller-Cochran, North Carolina State University; Emily H. Moorer, Hinds Community College; Diana Nystedt, Palo Alto College; Megan O'Neill, Stetson University; Victor Uszerowicz, Miami-Dade College; Sharon K. Walsh, Loyola University Chicago; and Cheryl A. Wilson, Indiana University of Pennsylvania.

Introduction

So who uses APA style? The APA (American Psychological Association) style of citation is the preferred form within the social or behavioral sciences and in the field of communications in the academic community. APA remains a valid form of documentation in all cases, but various disciplines, publications, and instructors prefer and expect different types of citation—others include MLA (Modern Language Association) style, CMS (the *Chicago Manual of Style*), and the Number System. The standard for citing legal documents and court rulings is *The Bluebook: A Uniform System of Citation*. Find out which specific style of citation is required for your research writing task before you begin.

APA documentation uses two main components: first, **reference citations in your text (in-text citations),** which are often in the form of **parenthetical citations,** to all outside sources you have consulted in writing your essay. Citations include a direct reference to the author(s) and the publication date, and also a page number or page range when using direct quotes. Internet sources without page numbers are a special case; see page 44. (We will refer to these reference citations as **in-text citations.**) Second, you must complete a **references list** that includes the full publishing information for each source. The citations within your text will correspond to the sources in your references list, which will appear at the end of your paper.

APA documentation is meant to be accessible and usable for both the writer and the reader. We think you'll agree, once you get comfortable with it, that most aspects of APA style are pretty easy to use. APA indicates sources of outside information clearly and immediately for your reader while saving you and the reader the difficulties of working through constant footnotes. Further, when you effectively document your sources as a research writer, you demonstrate authority and offer credible support for your ideas and position. Perhaps just as important, your documentation guides readers quickly and precisely to the sources you have gathered so that your readers might build on the concepts and issues introduced in your work. Proper documentation allows you to enter into a scholarly conversation that, ideally, goes well beyond any single essay.

Plagiarism and Academic Honesty

Plagiarism is an *extremely* serious issue in the academic world because our educational system is committed to protecting ethics and integrity in the transmission of information. Freedom of information and inquiry come with the obligation of academic honesty. Documentation styles such as APA exist not simply to provide technical guidelines for academic research, but also to help maintain the highest standards of academic honesty in all scholarly communications. All of us who write and present information within the academic world need to be clearly aware of the expectations and rules for integrating source material into our own writing and public presentations in order to uphold academic honesty. Understanding what type of information must be cited and then properly documenting all your sources are the keys to avoiding plagiarism, and this manual is designed to assist you in correctly documenting sources in the APA style.

Plagiarism negates any merit a student's paper or presentation may otherwise have had, damages irreparably the credibility of the perpetrator, limits the possibility for independent and critical thinking, diminishes the trust between teachers and students, and undermines the accomplishments of those who struggle and succeed through their own efforts. Plagiarism at its most severe is a form of fraud or theft, and the plagiarist is viewed as a thief and a cheat in scholarly circles as well as in the publishing industry. In some cases plagiarism breaks the law, but all forms of plagiarism constitute academic dishonesty and may subject a student to serious penalties. Much as with instances of copyright infringement, the stakes can be extremely high when money is involved, sometimes resulting in multimillion-dollar lawsuits. Penalties for students who have succumbed to the temptation to plagiarize in their academic work tend to be more modest, of course, ranging from a failing grade to institutional expulsion (policies differ among institutions, and you should familiarize yourself with your school's), but the results can be equally devastating for the offending party. Don't be tempted!

> *That's right: original words and ideas are considered forms of creative and intellectual property, and they are protected by law as such.*

Plagiarism has become increasingly easy to commit in the era of word processing and the Internet, and that makes the inducement even greater for some to take shortcuts. Most instructors, however, are attuned to the methods and stratagems typical of plagiarism and immediately recognize the stylistic differences between a student's scholarship and a professional's; they are also quite aware of the major ideas, arguments, and research in their fields. Like you, they use and know how to navigate the Internet, and they are aided by online plagiarism-detection services such as Turnitin.com, CheckForPlagiarism.net, and iThenticate.com. Sophistication in identifying plagiarism keeps pace with methods for accomplishing it. Again, don't be tempted!

All the information you present in a scholarly context that is not cited is assumed to be your words and ideas. "Forgetting" to cite a source you've used is akin to forgetting to pay for something at the mall—explaining to your professor that it was just an accident is like trying to explain to mall security how an unpaid-for CD got into your pocket. Presenting others' words, key ideas, or research findings without appropriate and complete acknowledgment, whatever the circumstances, whatever the intent, violates academic honesty.

The general expectation throughout the scholarly community is that all sources of information—except for those that provide what can be regarded as **common knowledge** (see the expanded definition in the Key Terms list in Chapter 3), such as standard dictionaries or encyclopedias—must be acknowledged and cited. The variety of source matter that must be cited includes, but is not limited to, the original content of all forms of verbal text (including literary, nonfiction, and technical writing); creative expression, output, structure, or design; original arguments or analyses along with their results or conclusions; original illustrative and graphic materials; and independently derived research and research findings.

This may sound potentially confusing, but the easy rule of thumb is to cite all your source material unless it is clearly common knowledge.

Plagiarism Defined

Most definitions of plagiarism emphasize two aspects:

1. The **direct** act of knowingly presenting another's words, creativity, research findings, or ideas as one's own in either exact or paraphrased form. In short, plagiarism in its most serious form involves falsely taking credit for someone else's thoughts and efforts.

2. Presenting others' words, key ideas, or research findings without appropriate and complete acknowledgment. Various types of **misattribution** might be a matter of error or oversight, but failing to set quotation marks around a directly quoted excerpt from another's work or omitting a correct citation, whatever the intent, constitutes plagiarism.

Direct Plagiarism

Copying and pasting from one or several sources, purchasing a complete essay from an online plagiarism mill, or "borrowing" an essay from a friend, even with that friend's permission, are typical examples of this sort of plagiarism if you submit the results as your own work. This remains true whether it is a matter of an entire paper or just a few sentences. It also remains true if you strategically intersperse plagiarized material with your own writing or if you combine and interweave a number of sources without proper documentation. While these types of plagiarism typically take the form of exact, **word-for-word** (**verbatim**) reproduction from a secondary source, such as might be readily found on the web, **paraphrasing** (putting another author's thoughts and ideas into your own words) is also plagiarism if the original source is not clearly or explicitly acknowledged. Remember, too, that the unique, distinctive structure of a source is protected along with its original concepts and ideas.

Misattribution and Plagiarism

The second category of plagiarism, **misattribution,** may well occur without a writer's intending to deceive the reader or appropriate the work of another. An oversight in the mechanics of acknowledging a reference source or the inadvertent omission of an acknowledgment or citation are examples of misattribution. Giving incorrect information about one's source can be defined as plagiarism under this category as well—again, regardless of the intent. While most professors are aware that honest mistakes can occur in documentation, the complete omission of a citation always casts doubts on the author's integrity.

A related issue is that of "fair use," which concerns the extent to which another source can be drawn on in one's own work. According to Turnitin.com, it is a violation of fair use standards to copy "so many words or ideas from a source that it makes up the majority of your work, whether you give credit or not"; similarly if you were to have assistance in editing your work to the extent that its essential structure, style, and "voice" no longer belonged to you, submitting it as your own would be an act of plagiarism.

Academic honesty promotes individual critical thinking along with a respect for and responsibility toward the work of others. Zero tolerance for plagiarism is a way of honoring students who work to attain these standards. And while this guide focuses on the APA style of documentation in writing, it is important to realize that the strictures against plagiarism apply with equal force when you convey information through PowerPoint® or another media- or graphic-based presentation format *or* in an oral delivery.

Examples of Plagiarism: Recognizing and Avoiding

The first, most blatant kind of plagiarism is frequently carried out when a student lifts some portion of an existing work—often by copying directly from a web-based source—and passes it off as her or his own. Direct plagiarism also occurs when exact words, ideas, and concepts are paraphrased (i.e., reworded but substantively identical), or even when a distinctive presentational structure is used without acknowledgment and under false pretense of ownership.

No matter how cleverly the concepts are reworked or reordered, if the author or source that originated them is not acknowledged, the result is plagiarism. Nor does it matter whether or not the plagiarized source is of particularly high quality or prestigious authorship. When used in your writing, another student's essay should be cited as surely as the Pulitzer Prize–winning source we draw on below. In the following example, both word-for-word and paraphrased excerpts from a popular history text are integrated with a hypothetical student's essay on race relations in New York. The plagiarized sections are underlined for clear identification.

Original Source Material

Burrows, E. G., & Wallace, M. (1999). *Gotham: A history of New York City to 1898*. New York, NY: Oxford University Press.

> New York radicals' boldest intervention in civic affairs involved political rather than physical reconstruction. In tandem with Republican initiatives in the South and other states, New York's radicals pressed for giving the black population the right to vote. African Americans, in their churches, newspapers, and state conventions, had been demanding the suffrage as a fair return for their war service, and many radicals agreed a debt was due. The elimination of the existing $250 property qualification, moreover, might add eleven thousand blacks to the rolls, virtually all of whom would vote Republican. This was a bloc of considerable consequence, given that Republican Governor Reuben Fenton had won by only eight thousand votes in 1864 and that Democratic presidential candidate Horace Seymour would carry the state by just nine thousand votes in 1868. The bulk of these potential Republicans, moreover, lived in the Democratic strongholds of New York City and Brooklyn.

Word-for-Word Plagiarism

> The so-called *radicals* of New York worked <u>with Republican initiatives in the South</u> to give <u>the black population the right to vote</u>. African Americans <u>had been demanding the suffrage</u> rights <u>as a fair return for their war service</u>, and most radicals agreed with them. Republicans could make great political gains by enfranchising blacks and by eliminating the <u>existing $250 property qualification,</u> which <u>might add eleven thousand blacks to the rolls.</u> This would give the Republicans inroads into <u>the Democratic strongholds of New York City and Brooklyn.</u>

Plagiarism Through Paraphrase

We have omitted underlining here because the excerpt is *entirely* plagiarized:

> The so-called "radicals" of New York worked with southern Republicans to give the blacks the right to vote. African Americans claimed the right to vote because of their role in the Civil War, and most radicals agreed with them. Republicans could make great political gains by enfranchising blacks and by eliminating the property qualifications, which would add thousands of black voters to the Republican roster. This would give the Republicans inroads into the Democratic bastions of the New York City metropolitan area.

And finally, here is a validly documented version, combining direct quote and appropriately cited paraphrase. Please note that the paraphrased version above could be properly cited by beginning: "According to Burrows and Wallace (1999)…"

Properly Cited Version

> Burrows and Wallace (1999) examine racial politics during the Reconstruction phase after the Civil War. African Americans argued that they had earned voting rights through their military contributions during the war, and most so-called New York *radicals* agreed with them. They needed to work in "tandem with Republican initiatives in the South," however, to give "the black population the right to vote" (p. 926). Republicans stood to make great political gains by eliminating a long-standing property-holding requirement ($250) for voting, which "might add eleven thousand blacks to the rolls," many of whom resided within what were then "the Democratic strongholds of New York City and Brooklyn" (p. 926).

Other kinds of plagiarism involve the use of others' research findings or personal experiences without giving due credit. Again, it is vital to remember that plagiarism does not refer only to exact words: an author's unique conclusions, research, and style of presentation are all protected intellectual property as well. In some cases plagiarism breaks the law, but all forms of plagiarism constitute academic dishonesty and may subject a student to serious penalties.

The examples below emphasize statistical information that, while factual rather than interpretive in nature, does not belong to the arena of **common knowledge** and must therefore be cited. They again demonstrate both **word-for-word** and **paraphrased** plagiarism from a book by Jared Diamond, and again, the plagiarized sections are underlined for clear identification. The plagiarized paraphrase is entirely stolen, despite the rewording.

Original Source Material

Diamond, J. (2005). *Collapse: How societies choose to fail or succeed.* New York, NY: Viking Penguin.

> In 1992, eight years after the state of Colorado had issued an operating permit to Galactic Resources, the company declared bankruptcy and closed the mine on less

than a week's notice, leaving a large local tax bill unpaid, laying off its employees, stopping essential environmental maintenance, and abandoning the site. A few months later, after the start of the winter snowfalls, the heap-leach system overflowed, sterilizing an 18-mile stretch of the Alamosa River with cyanide. It was then discovered that the state of Colorado had required a financial guarantee of only $4,500,000 from Galactic Resources as a condition for issuing the permit, but that cleanup would cost $180,000,000. After the government had extracted another $28,000,000 as part of the bankruptcy settlement, taxpayers were left to pay $147,500,000 through the Environmental Protection Agency.

Word-for-Word Plagiarism

In 1992 Galactic Resources declared bankruptcy and closed their mine leaving a large local tax bill unpaid, and abandoning the site. A few months later the maintenance system overflowed, polluting an 18-mile stretch of the Alamosa River with cyanide. Colorado had required a financial guarantee of only $4,500,000 from Galactic Resources, but the cleanup would cost $180,000,000, of which taxpayers had to pay $147,500,000.

Plagiarism Through Paraphrase

Western states have not required sufficient financial guarantees for environmental cleanup from mining corporations. For example, the mining company Galactic Resources was required to guarantee only $4,500,000 for cleanup by the state of Colorado, but when they filed for bankruptcy the state was able to get back only about $28,000,000, leaving the Environmental Protection Agency with a bill of $147,500,000, which taxpayers had to fund.

Properly Cited Paraphrase with Word-for-Word Quotation

Diamond (2005) argues that western states have not required sufficient financial guarantees for environmental cleanup from mining corporations. For example, the mining company Galactic Resources was required to guarantee only $4,500,000 for cleanup by the state of Colorado, but when they filed for bankruptcy the state was able to recoup only another $28,000,000, leaving taxpayers "to pay $147,500,000 through the Environmental Protection Agency" (p. 457).

Our emphatic and pointed discussion of academic honesty is not intended to intimidate or frighten our student readers. Most teaching faculty do not relish the role of acting as plagiarism cops; many, in fact, find it the saddest of necessities. We recognize that the vast majority of students work extremely hard to achieve their educational success and to become accomplished, responsible, independent thinkers. Understanding what type of information must be cited and then properly documenting all your sources are the keys to avoiding plagiarism, and this manual is designed to assist you in mastering the basics of the APA documentation style.

2

Finding and Evaluating Sources

The Physical Library

For many generations of students, the campus library has afforded not only a quiet, comfortable place to study and undertake research, but also a special aura and atmosphere that lingers fondly in their memories when they recall their college days. In this "information age," however, many students would rather go online than go to the library—not an unreasonable preference considering the constantly improving range and number of databases, online publications, and reliable web sources available. Nonetheless, the physical library hasn't been rendered obsolete on the college campus just yet. Ignoring the print texts in your library, as well as the additional access to specialized and subscription databases a library provides, seriously limits the pool of reliable, nearby sources available to you. The operative term here is *reliable*. We now use the word "google" as a generic verb for conducting a web search, but Google™ is a commercial vehicle, and it is designed with a commercial agenda. Although it seems a no-brainer to say it, you will dramatically increase your effectiveness as a researcher by familiarizing yourself with your local library's physical resources, which include specific subject sections, documents and archives, and even the librarians themselves. Your online searches will also be enhanced by the increased access to scholarly databases you get by browsing your library's search engine and by learning how to refine your searches and maximize their relevance to your needs.

The following are library services with which you should be familiar.

Reference Librarian

One of the most valuable resources for a student learning to use the library is the reference librarian. A living, breathing professional who can answer most questions on the spot is something no electronic database can offer. But because reference librarians are often very busy (even harried at certain times of the day), the more focused and specific you can make your questions, the better. Many libraries offer free classes, organized and taught by librarians, on how to use the library. Others offer introductory tours on an individual basis. Check out the options at your library.

Library Catalog

Almost all American libraries now use computerized catalogs, yet this electronic resource is your essential guide to the print texts at your disposal. You can search by author and title of a work, but unless you already have a clear idea of what sources you need, subject or keyword searches may be your best option. A subject search draws on the Library of Congress subject headings that have become the standard for classifying and organizing college library holdings. A keyword search can be a versatile tool, but, as with using a typical Internet search engine, patience and resourcefulness on your part may be necessary. The first terms you input will not always lead you to the best sources—you may get too many "hits," thus requiring you to narrow the search using more specific or fewer terms, which then requires the use of broader (or even different) terms. We recommend that you prepare a list of search terms in advance and plan to go to **the stacks** to examine potential texts to assess their relevance and usefulness for your project. The catalog provides a brief set of bibliographic details on each text along with its location in the form of a **call number**—carefully write this down!

Reference Section

This section, which is nearly always on the main floor of a library quite near circulation, houses a vast repository of encyclopedias, dictionaries, compilations of facts, statistical data, bibliographies, lists, atlases, rankings, etc. Specific areas within the reference section are devoted to specific disciplines or categories, and it is worth your time to learn the reference holdings for your major as well as for the fields covered within your other course work.

The Stacks

The forest of bookshelves in a large library can be a bit intimidating, but the collections are arranged by subject, and only a few sections will be devoted to your discipline or current area of study. Locating the specific areas associated with your major can pay big dividends. Once you've found a few sources in the **library catalog** that match your topic, you can cruise the stacks in that region to see what else is there. This can often turn up more appropriate sources than an extensive catalog search that may lack the most appropriate or compatible search terms.

Current Journals and Other Periodicals

Libraries generally subscribe to a variety of newspapers, popular magazines, and scholarly journals, which they place on current-reading shelves for a certain period of time and then either store within the stacks or archive in some other way. Don't disregard this tremendously useful category of publications. Until a much greater percentage of reputable periodicals publish regularly online, bound periodical collections, particularly **scholarly journals,** will remain among the most valuable resources available to the student researcher. Scholarly journals tend to be more current and digestible than the typical scholarly **monograph** (a book-length study), and, in fact, it is common for a major scholarly concept or argument to see publication as a journal article before it reaches full elaboration in an independent volume. Many disciplines also combine articles on related topics within particular **issues,** and you will often find reviews of recent texts that have relevance to your own current investigation. While they lack the rigorous quality controls of their scholarly counterparts, other types of periodicals can also be beneficial sources, owing to their immediacy and their capacity to reflect the world beyond academic circles. Because of the sheer physical bulk of so many periodicals in their original print medium, however, many libraries are shifting to electronic formats for storage. One such format is on microfiche, which allows for far more compact storage but requires a special machine for reading it. It is definitely in your best interests to find out how your library stores the journals germane to your major or current research project.

Other Services

Modern college libraries often offer a wide range of services beyond housing and providing access to texts, such as writing labs, video collections and players, interlibrary loan options, group study space, copying centers, conference rooms—the list goes on and on, and it varies with each library. Find out what special services your library offers.

The Electronic Library

While virtually all college libraries now have computer terminals dedicated to searching for information of all kinds, an even more convenient service many libraries offer is that of allowing you to browse through their search engines and databases from your personal computer. One helpful feature of remote access to online databases is the increasing availability of "full-text" which you can locate and download from the comfort of your own home or dorm room. The range of sources any library can hold has been increased exponentially by online databases, but most require paid subscriptions and would not be available to you if you were not working through your library's search engine, typically accessed through the library's home page.

The variety of specialized databases available today can easily overwhelm and frustrate an unprepared student researcher; therefore, it is important to know the best databases for researching a given topic. Chances are your library will subscribe to some or all of the following databases. This selective list is useful for a general search of popular newspapers, magazines, multidisciplinary journals, government publications, encyclopedias, as well as online sources.

General Search

Academic Search Premier—a multidisciplinary academic database, some full text.

Article First—gives multidisciplinary journal article citations.

Books in Print—the best source for in-print, out-of-print, and forthcoming books.

GPO—Government Publication Index.

Ingenta—tables of contents for a wide range of journals.

JSTOR—offers full text for scholarly journals.

MasterFile Premier—many full-text, multidisciplinary offerings.

NationalNewspaper—a wide range of full-text American newspapers.

Newspaper Source—a wide range of full-text international newspapers.

ProQuest Direct—a range of interdisciplinary journals, some full text.

Topic Search—a current-events database.

Discipline-Specific Searches

Arts and Humanities (Selected Databases)

American History and Life—an index to American history articles in all eras.

Communication and Mass Media Complete—a major index for communication arts.

Contemporary Literary Criticism Select—contemporary literary criticism.

Dictionary of Literary Biography—biographical and critical essays.

Historical Abstracts—world history index from 1450 to the present.

MLA—Modern Language Association indexes (literature, language, linguistics, etc.).

Oxford English Dictionary—the most authoritative and complete English dictionary.

Philosopher's Index—a major index for philosophy students.

Religion and Philosophy Collection—an index for world religions and philosophy.

World History Abstracts—indexes and abstracts for world history.

Business and Law (Selected Databases)

ABI/INFORM Trade & Industry—a wide range of business-related indexes.

Business Source Premier—indexes of scholarly business journals.

EconLit—indexes for economic journals.

EDGAR—Securities and Exchange filings and information.

Find Law—directory of web-based legal resources.

HeinOnline—a full-text collection of legal research material.

Industry Norms and Key Business Ratios—key business information.

Regional Business News—a full-text collection of U.S. business news.

Test Locator & Test Review—test and research information.

Education (Selected Databases)

eLibrary Elementary—a database geared toward K–6 students.
ERIC—a key educational resource, with citations and abstracts.
K-12—searches a range of databases for information geared to a young audience.
Mas Ultra—a database aimed at high school students' interests.
Professional Development—indexes to core educational journals.
SPORTDiscus—a full-text research tool for school athletics.
Test Locator & Test Review—test and research information.

Engineering and Applied Sciences (Selected Databases)

ACM Digital Library—Association of Computing Machinery online resources.
Agricola—indexes for agricultural literature.
Computer Source—full-text computer science articles.
Ei Engineering Village—Compendex Engineering Index and other indexes.
IEEE—full text of IEEE (Institute of Electrical and Electronics Engineers) journals.

Nursing and Medicine (Selected Databases)

Alt HealthWatch—coverage of alternative medicine sources.
CINAHL—Cumulative Index to Nursing and Allied Health.
Clinical Pharmacology—up-to-date pharmacology sources.
Health Source: Nursing/Academic—full-text scholarly journals.
ICN Union List of Journals—index to health sciences journals.
Medline—health sciences database sponsored by the National Library of Medicine.
PubMed—accesses Medline and other biomedical sources.
PubMed Central—a subset of full-text articles from the PubMed database.
Stat!Ref—full-text health-care reference resources.

Sciences (Selected Databases)

ACS Publications—full-text American Chemical Society publications.
Agricola—indexes for agricultural literature.
CRC Handbook—handbook of chemistry and physics.
Ebsco Animals—information related to biology.
Institute of Physics—online access to *Journal of Physics*.
MathSciNet—access to mathematical reviews.
PROLA—Physical Review online.
SciFinder Scholar—chemical abstracts online.
SPORTDiscus—a full-text research tool for school athletics.

Social and Behavioral Sciences (Selected Databases)

APA—American Psychological Association.
CIAO—Columbia International Affairs Online, political science sources.
Communication and Mass Media Complete—a major index for communication studies.
CQ Weekly—current congressional issues.

CultureGrams—cultural and sociological information.
National Criminal Justice Reference Service Abstracts—an index to criminology sources.
PsychiatryOnline—an important resource from the American Psychiatric Association.
PsycINFO—a vast archive of citations published by the APA.
Psychology and Behavioral Sciences Collection—indexes to topics of concern within the field.
Social Services Abstracts—indexes and abstracts for social science journals.
SocINDEX—a full-text social sciences index.
SPORTDiscus—a full-text research tool for school athletics.

Other Sources

A great many of the sources held in libraries and databases are **secondary sources** (with literary works being the large exception), but primary sources acquired through your own efforts and ingenuity can also be quite valuable. Interviews, lab research, unpublished diaries, and self-conducted surveys (to list only a few examples) can add a great deal to a research paper. For example, if you have a relative who is an administrator at a hospital, and you find yourself researching the current shortage of qualified nurses, interviewing that person could add an authoritative, specifically focused voice to your argument. Be creative in your research, and consider all your available resources.

Evaluating Print Sources

A full discussion of research methodology is beyond the scope of this text, but the following is a thumbnail sketch of how to rate potential source material. Finding source material, often way more than you can use, is fairly easy for most subjects. Determining which sources are the most appropriate and reliable for your project may be the greatest challenge—but for many, also the greatest reward—involved with a scholarly endeavor. A common pitfall confronting the inexperienced or overeager researcher is the impulse simply to "grab" the first few likely looking and easily available sources from the first page of a long list. Time constraints will often be an important limiting factor in your research, restricting you to readily available choices (such as full-text online sources, holdings in your library, etc.). If you begin early and plan ahead, however, you can gain access to a far wider range of source material. Leave yourself time to sort through the likely prospects to determine which are most suitable for your project and to gather more difficult-to-get sources by other means, such as requesting a book through interlibrary loan, spooling through microfiche, conducting firsthand primary research (fieldwork), or even going to other local libraries.

Evaluating by Author, Publisher, and Date

Our discussion of source evaluation will focus predominantly on **secondary** rather than **primary** sources. A brief refresher: a **primary source** is an item of direct, immediate evidence whereas a **secondary source** is an analysis or interpretation in response to primary matter. A useful distinction might be drawn from the field of archaeology, where cultural artifacts comprise much of the primary source matter. The fact of the arti*fact*—a shard of pottery, an inscription in a tomb, a ceremonial mask—is its existence; the archaeologist's job (once authenticity has been established) is to place the artifact within a context in order to interpret and reach conclusions about its function, meaning, or significance, the written results of which would be developed and circulated as a secondary source. Undergraduate APA users deal mostly with secondary sources, and therefore must determine what array of secondary sources will best enable them to conduct their own scholarly act of interpretation and analysis. When it comes to secondary sources, not all are created equally, and the fact of their existence does not automatically establish their validity or reliability.

As we discuss more fully in Chapter 3, APA requires whenever possible a citation for each source, which includes at least the author, publisher, and date of publication. These vital statistics aid readers in easily locating the cited sources for themselves, but they also comprise the vital factors a scholar considers when determining the merits of a potential source. An easy-to-remember evaluative strategy is to subject a potential secondary source to the four C's: **credibility, collegiality, currency,** and **context.**

The **author** profile is the single most important determinant of the viability of a scholarly source—therefore, be sure to scrutinize each potential author according to the four C's. What level of **credibility** does the author under consideration have? What credentials and established expertise has he or she demonstrated within the relevant field of study? Consider such things as educational background, professional assignments and affiliations, other publications or achievements in the field, and even awards or honors. Don't be wowed by titles alone: they can be misleading. A cardiovascular surgeon who decides to write about the Civil War may not have the historiographic knowledge and skills to do so in a credible manner despite having earned the right to be referred to as a doctor in the world of medicine. Particularly if the author is not a professional scholar, consider also the apparent purpose of the source. Let's face it: books by political candidates released at the height of a closely contested campaign have an intent other than the neutral, objective sharing of information. Corporate authors too should be critically assessed. A long-standing and prestigious organization such as the NAACP has more automatic and immediate credibility than the recently incorporated AntiAging Institute, even though both have undeniable agendas.

In offering the term **collegiality,** we encourage you to consider the extent to which the source and its author are situated within a larger dialogue among experts in that area. How completely does your author ground her argument and investigation among a variety of diverse and interesting sources generated by colleagues and peers? What is the range and abundance of sources the author cites? An author who offers little but an individual perspective, no matter how qualified an expert she might be, will likely be of less use and value to your project than an author who provides you a comprehensive familiarity with a broad spectrum of research and expertise on a particular topic or issue. How completely has your author shown **currency** through displaying a great awareness of recent and ongoing research, and what new, compelling data is made available within the source? How recently was the source published? Has its content been superseded or severely contested by more current work? Finally, what is the **context** for the source—meaning, under what circumstances and in what environment was the source generated, and within what framework do you hope to use it? Certainly, context overlaps with the first three C's, but in some situations, considering context might help you to see a valid use for a source that you might otherwise be inclined to disregard. For example, a source written in 1980 might initially seem to lack the **currency** you need for your essay on steroid use among contemporary athletes, but because of the **context** in which it was written, it could help to illustrate the relationship between social awareness and usage, an avenue you hadn't thought to explore previously.

> **A Helpful Suggestion:** Scholarly sources thoroughly document their own extensive sources of information, so locating even one that particularly fits your project can provide a cornucopia of other resources more valuable than any nonscholarly source brings to your undertaking. So why not start there?

A source's **publisher** is also an important indicator of reliability, and some publishers definitely have more credibility than others. As an extreme example from the category of periodicals, an article in *The Economist* about the possible effects of speculators on oil prices would have a much higher level of reliability than a speculative article in *The Star* on the existence of Bigfoot (and believe it or not, Bigfoot is a subject of academic study), despite the fact that both are newspaper opinion pieces. The most reliable sources in a specific field frequently come from academic presses and journals. Major organizations such as the American Psychological Association (APA), the American Chemical Society (ACS), and the Modern Language Association (MLA), to name only a few, generally publish the leading journal in their respective fields, and they also provide indexes to scholarly journals. **Scholarly journals** are very carefully edited for verifiable content, proper attribution and use of sources, and quality of contribution to the respective fields they cover. They contain articles by professionals and experts, whose status and reputations rely on their credibility. Since they are generally **peer reviewed,** which means that other experts read and critique all submissions before they are accepted or rejected, these journals are exceptionally collegial by their very nature. This high level of professionalism in article selection and editing makes scholarly journals among the most reliable secondary sources. Though they seldom match the currency of journalistic periodicals and many web publications—they are often published quarterly (or even less frequently)—scholarly journals tend to demonstrate that instant gratification can be at odds with reliability and that **context** can trump currency. Seldom will you see a leading scholarly journal forced to print a retraction owing to an error in reporting or an ill-considered and sensationalistic statement. These journals nevertheless achieve an immediacy and currency far greater than **monographs** and classroom textbooks while maintaining a comparable degree of scholarly integrity.

Most books circulated by successful publishers undergo extensive editing, but those monographs coming out of academic presses (usually designated as

"University Press" on the title page) also undergo peer review and tend to reflect the work of authors with high credibility and well-established expertise. A scholarly monograph can never match the currency of a scholarly journal because the quality-control measures of monographs take commensurately longer for longer works (and because, in honesty, the wheels of academic publication can turn rather slowly), yet the greater scale and scope allow for even more extensive collegiality. The date of publication is important, as we have discussed, but is more critical in some disciplines than in others. For example, a critical examination of Emily Dickinson's poetry from the 1960s might still be quite relevant, while a computer science text from the same time period would be woefully behind the times, perhaps even laughable, because of the technological advances in the field. Questions of context run parallel for both forms of scholarly media, particularly in light of the fact that the typical monograph has seen portions of its study published in article form within a scholarly journal while being completed.

In the arena of book publishing, texts released by independent **educational presses** stand next in the hierarchy of reliability. You may already be familiar with some of the major names: Pearson, Prentice-Hall, W. W. Norton & Co., Viking Penguin, and Bedford/St. Martin's are among the heavy hitters in the industry. These publishers, who produce texts mainly for student use, share a close relationship with the academic world, a relationship that demands a high level of credibility in their publications, and their quality-control standards are accordingly more rigorous than those of their trade/mass-market counterparts. Many prospective publications from educational presses undergo a process of peer review and subsequent revision to help ensure standards of both credibility and collegiality, which, again, impacts currency. Trade publishers, on the other hand, whose products are mostly what you see filling the shelves, tables, and displays of any mainstream bookstore, have vastly different target audiences and much different standards from those of publishers with an academic orientation. Their goal is to sell books in the greatest possible quantities, and aside from protecting themselves from culpability in plagiarism, they tend to circulate texts under the credo of *caveat emptor,* "buyer beware." Trade publications require neither collegiality nor often credibility in authorship, and despite the fact that they frequently exceed academic and educational publications in terms of currency, that seeming advantage is not so great that it should be a decisive factor in your choice. There are without question useful, credible sources available through trade publishers, but the onus falls more completely on the reader to scrutinize the author and the style in which the text is presented.

> **A Helpful Reminder:** If you are in doubt about the merits of a particular source, consult your reference librarian or, if appropriate, your instructor. Don't disregard your human resources in your quest for textual ones.

Evaluating Online Sources

Who publishes, or sponsors, a **web site** is as important a consideration as who publishes or sponsors print sources and often can be determined from the **domain name** when not indicated elsewhere. Most of the "gold standard" professional organizations listed above (APA, ACS, etc.) have web sites helpful for finding good online and print sources, and it is well worth visiting the sites most pertinent to your field of study. The Internet was originated, not by Al Gore, but by scientists seeking a vehicle for regular and open communications, and that spirit lives on in many ways. Web postings allow for an accessible immediacy not possible with any other public medium; their currency can be in real time in some instances. The web offers a wealth of uncensored, free, and open information that persists despite efforts to commercialize or regulate its flow, and the technology of hyper-textual links allows for an extreme degree of collegiality. For all their abundance, variety, immediacy, and accessibility, however, online sources can present special problems because, to understate the case, many are not as carefully edited and reviewed as their print counterparts—anybody can put any opinion he or she wants on a web site or even post misinformation intentionally. The democratization of information thus doesn't automatically equate to increased reliability. Another difficulty online sources present is that the web is constantly changing, and a site that is accessible today may be gone tomorrow, or may have been updated without warning to a newer version. Sometimes a source can exist online in several different states of "update" at one time. Nonetheless, more and more great online sources are appearing every day, and the web is fast becoming an essential venue for all disciplines. One way to begin to evaluate an online source is to take a close look at its **Uniform Resource Locator (URL).** Even when a DOI (the APA's preferred locator) is available, the URL can still tell you much about the source. This is the "address" that appears when you access a web site, and it contains a lot of valuable information for determining the source's reliability, most notably in the domain name and **extension.**

http://www.americanheart.org/presenter.jhtml?identifier=3053

Protocol   Domain Name   Extension   Document Path   File name/Identifier

Protocol

This tells the browser software what method of data transfer to use to access the information on that particular site. The abbreviation "http" stand for "hypertext transfer protocol," "https" for "hypertext transfer protocol secure," and "ftp" for "file transfer protocol." The symbols "://" separate the protocol from the domain name.

Domain Name

Technically, this simply identifies the name of the server where the source material resides, but it is often the address for an organization's home page, and will sometimes identify a corporate author as the source when no author is listed. For example, the URL listed above will take you to a page entitled "Heart Attack/Stroke Warning Signs," which has no listed author. The American Heart Association can be assigned as the author of this article because the article is part of the list of links the Association claims as its own on its home page, and that attribution also appears in the URL. The home page also provides links to other sites (and therefore to other authors), which are clearly labeled both in the link and in the new URL. As with print sources, establishing authorship is crucial to gauging credibility.

Domain Extension

The domain extension can be very useful when quickly scanning for reliable sites because it indicates the general purpose of the site host, the equivalent of the publisher in this medium. For example, ".org" and ".edu" extensions are reserved for nonprofit and educational institutions, respectively. While such designations do not guarantee the quality of a source, these sites are web havens for reliable authors and institutions, and will be most likely to offer the benefits of scholarly collegiality. Likewise, the extensions ".gov" and ".mil" designate government and military sites, and carry the nominative reliability of the respective agency responsible for the site. Sites with ".com" or ".biz" extensions are business enterprises, and may be more interested in advertising a particular product than in providing reliable information. The ".net" designation is generally for private use.

Document Path and File Name or Identifier

The last portion of the URL leads to the desired document and file, and it is case sensitive (meaning you have to be careful with capitalization). It is easier to cut and paste a long URL than to retype it. If you need to cite a URL and the document path portion is very long, it is best to cite the domain home page URL rather than reproduce an overlengthy identifier.

3

Citing Sources in Academic Writing

Key Terms

Block Quote An exactly quoted excerpt of more than 40 words. (Quotations of 40 or fewer words should be enclosed in quotation marks and integrated into your text.) Block quotes must be set apart from your own text by indenting the entire quote five spaces, or one half-inch, from the left margin. Spacing for block quotes should follow the spacing in the main body of your paper (generally double-spaced). The concluding punctuation for a block quote comes before the parenthetical citation. See next page.

Citation A specific reference to a source that has produced a particular quote, concept, creative work, argument, statistic, analysis, or graphic material integrated into or referred to in a scholarly work; or, the process of systematically creating such references. Citations are forms of acknowledgment or attribution.

Common Knowledge

1. Information considered throughout the mainstream of the academic world to be of a factual nature and so generally agreed upon as to belong to the realm of what "everybody knows" (or perhaps what everybody should know), such as would be presented without qualification in a standard dictionary or encyclopedia: for example, that a noun is a naming word for living beings, places, objects, and actions; that the earth is in orbit around the sun; that Thomas Alva Edison developed the first viable incandescent light

bulb. By contrast, specialized and rarely presented facts, such as the heart rate of an African crown eagle or the favorite book of Abraham Lincoln, should be attributed to a particular source of information. Because it is generally known and accepted, common knowledge will appear in numerous sources and will essentially be taken for granted; thus it requires no citation or attribution in most instances as long as you state it in your *own words*.

2. A well-known quote or saying (proverb), such as "beauty is in the eye of the beholder" or "love is blind." Many of the phrases in this category are considered clichés, however, and should appear in your writing rarely, only when they most aptly express what the situation calls for.

Concluding Punctuation   Punctuation that concludes a sentence can be a period (.), a question mark (?), or an exclamation point (!). As a general rule, concluding punctuation for a sentence comes *after* the parenthetical citation: (Author, date, p. #). You should, however, keep an exclamation point or question mark that ends a direct quote attached to the quote, and (like a comma or period) it should fall inside the quotation marks; for example, "Koff (2004) wonders 'can it happen here?'" (p. 203). Note that in these special circumstances, there is redundant concluding punctuation. Concluding punctuation for a block quote follows more standard rules, and the parenthetical citation is placed outside it without additional punctuation added (see page 25).

Direct Quote   An exact, word-for-word (verbatim) excerpt from another's work set off by quotation marks ("quote") or in block quote format in your writing. Be careful to quote accurately and fairly (in the proper context).

Documentation   The **scholarly** process of carefully acknowledging your sources. The MLA style attempts to keep source citations streamlined in the main body of your text through parenthetical citations and to have each **in-text citation** correspond clearly to a full description of the **source** in the **works cited** section.

In-text Citation   A brief reference (consisting of the author's last name, year of publication, and frequently a page number), to a source within the body of a scholarly work that will be more fully described in the **references** section. The APA style of **documentation** places parentheses around any of this information that is not part of your running text. The forthcoming examples show a variety of ways to accomplish this.

Paraphrase   To put source's words, ideas, research, or conclusions into your own words. This is a completely valid way of presenting another **source** in your work, as long as you cite the original source and are careful to represent it accurately.

Parenthetical Citation   The MLA's economical system for labeling sources, primarily through author name and page number placed in parentheses. Parenthetical citations are used for both quoted and paraphrased material that is *directly* used in support of or as evidence within the body of the written text (as opposed to a consulted work or source that is never specifically referenced). See the range of examples in the following section.

References   The various items in the alphabetical list of sources at the end of your work that correspond to each **in-text citation** within the main body of your essay, report, or presentation. Each reference includes a full description of the **source:** author(s), date, title(s), editor(s), translator(s), edition, publishing data. In some cases you will also need to identify the medium (print, web, photograph, etc.). The second half of this guide deals with the many variables of creating a proper "References" section.

Scholarship　The research-based activities and products associated with professionals and students who participate in the broader academic conversation. Scholarly writing uses accepted documentation styles to acknowledge and credit its sources of information and to guide readers clearly and quickly toward those sources.

Source　An informational resource; any text, web site, artwork, chart, map, report, lecture, or interview that contributes to a scholarly project. Sources provide evidence, support, background, and authority. Sources are typically divided into two categories: **primary** and **secondary** sources.

> **primary source**—a direct item of evidence pertaining to the subject under discussion; or, in the case of literary and artistic criticism, the actual "text" being critiqued. Other examples of primary sources include information from an experiment you conducted, data from a survey you administered, or (in most cases) a historical document you retrieved from an archive.
>
> **secondary source**—external, after-the-fact commentary, research, or analysis relevant to your topic and particular position. Secondary sources will generally make up the bulk of sources undergraduates are asked to use, as they provide access to the expertise of professionals in any given field and allow you to benefit from the sum total of previous research in the area. For example, in an essay about class distinctions in *Twelfth Night,* Shakespeare's play would be a primary source, as would commentary on class issues by one of his contemporaries or a woodcut bearing a scene illustrating the concept. By contrast, a modern article by Anne Barton on the subject would be a secondary source. When you write a research paper for a college course, you add a secondary source to the pool of resources available in the world of information.

Summary　As a kind of comprehensive **paraphrase,** a summary briefly condenses another author's main points into an overview or synopsis. As with paraphrase, it is important to carefully and accurately represent the original **source.**

In-text Citations and the Three Rules of Form and Format

Why Document Sources Parenthetically?

You could get around the necessity of parenthetical citation and a references section altogether if you incorporated complete source information into your own text at all points, but this would become awkward and cumbersome (and unacceptable in most venues). Compare the two citations below. The first uses parenthetical citation, and the second eschews it for full in-text information:

Diamond (1999) claims that a "suitable starting point from which to compare historical developments on the different continents is around 11,000 B.C." (p. 35).

Jared Diamond claims in 1999 on page 35 of *Guns, Germs, and Steel: The Fates of Human Societies*, published by W. W. Norton of New York, that a "suitable starting point from which to compare historical developments on the different continents is around 11,000 B.C."

APA in-text citation streamlines source identification and documentation for the writer and the reader.

Once again, the primary goal of **in-text citation** is to inform your readers concisely of the sources that contribute to your research and allow them to match a citation to full publication information in your **references list.** A citation will generally consist of the author's last name (surname) and the year in which the source you refer to was published. When both items are included within the parentheses, the author reference comes first, followed by a comma and one space, and then the year of publication in full. The reader can match this information with your alphabetized list of all authors at the end of your paper to find the complete source reference.

1. A Work by One Author

If this information is directly presented in your text, and only one work by this author is referenced, no additional citation is necessary:

In 1999, Diamond proposed that divergences between human societies became significant only beginning about 11,000 B.C.E.

Parenthetical citations in APA style are allowed to "float" within a sentence so that they are connected as clearly as possible to the information, research, or findings they represent. For example, if you used information from the Jared Diamond work cited above, a parenthetical **in-text citation** would typically take one of these two forms:

Important divergences between human societies became significant beginning about 11,000 B.C.E. (Diamond, 1999).

Diamond (1999) shows how divergences between human societies became significant beginning about 11,000 B.C.E.

In the first example, the author is not mentioned in the text, so the full citation with the author's name goes at the end of the sentence. In the second instance, because the author's name is given in the sentence, the parenthetical citation of the year of publication immediately follows the author's name. This should be the case wherever an author is mentioned within the sentence. For example:

Though there were divergences among human societies even earlier, Diamond (1999) feels that they became especially significant beginning about 11,000 B.C.E.

Again, every in-text citation should lead the reader to a specific item in the **references list,** where all your sources will be listed alphabetically, and which will come after the main body of your essay. Take a moment to look over the sample essay on pages 33–40 to see how in-text citations work in conjunction with the references page. The Diamond source would appear this way in the references list:

> Diamond, J. (1999). *Guns, germs, and steel: The fates of human societies*. New York, NY: Norton.

In many cases you will want to directly quote your source, and in those instances, you must give the precise page number(s) on which the original appears.

> Diamond (1999) claims that the approximate date of 11,000 B.C.E. gives us a "suitable starting point from which to compare historical developments on the different continents" (p. 35).

APA also allows for and encourages you to specify a particular chapter of a longer work, abbreviating it in this way:

> Latour (1993, Chapter 4) outlines a strategy for applying a socially conscious form of "relativism" to the field of anthropology.

2. Multiple Sources in a Single Sentence

If you refer to multiple sources within the same sentence, each source needs to be cited clearly and separately.

> While Foster (1979) is most concerned with the ways Christian tradition helped shape literary ideas for American slave narratives, it can also be seen as an inspiration for direct action and even rebellion (Genovese, 1979).

Clarity should always be your overriding concern. Don't load up your sentences with citations unnecessarily, and use appropriate grammar to incorporate sources and references. On the other hand, don't avoid integrating sources just because they might overlap:

> In his famous *Narrative* (1982), Douglass denounces the use of Biblical scripture to endorse slavery, but Genovese (1979) and Foster (1979) show that Christianity could also provide empowering ideas and even help stir resistance or rebellion.

3. Punctuating and Formatting Citations

Mechanics and punctuation follow a few special rules in APA style, and the following guidelines should see you through most situations.

Separate elements of each reference cited within parentheses are separated by commas. When all three possible elements are included, the sequence runs author(s), year of publication, and page number, as in this example:

> The popular spread of early rhythm and blues music of the '50s was hampered by "the rapid turnover of artists working in the field" (Dates & Barlow, 1990, p. 68).

Two or more references within the same parenthetical citation are alphabetized and separated by semicolons:

> (Tannahill, 1980; Tuchman, 1978)

Parenthetical citations take no independent punctuation. In other words, insert them as closely as possible to the source referenced, and punctuate the sentence as you normally would. In the Douglass citation on page 24, for instance, the first comma is there not because of the reference to a publication year but because of the structure of the opening clause. You'll notice that neither the Genovese nor the Foster citation receives any additional punctuation. When the parenthetical citation comes at the end of a sentence, the period follows it to keep the citation within the sentence. (If a direct quote ends with an exclamation point (!) or a question mark (?), that punctuation falls inside the quotation marks.)

Block Quotes and Embedded Quotes

Block Quotes

Quotes of 40 words or fewer should be directly integrated into your text set within standard quotation marks. Block quotes are quoted excerpts of more than 40 words, which must be set apart from your own text by indenting the entire quote five spaces, or one half-inch, from the left margin. Spacing for block quotes should follow the spacing in the main body of your paper (generally double-spacing). Do not use quotation marks within a block quote, but do cite the page number, which in this case will follow concluding punctuation:

> Jameson (1990) notes:
>
> infinity in this sense, this new grey placelessness, as well as what prepares it, also bears another familiar name. It is in Forster's imperialism, or Empire, to give it its period designation. It is Empire which stretches the roads out to infinity, beyond the bounds and the borders of the national state. (p. 323)

While a block quote is set off by indentation rather than quotation marks, there may be quotation marks within the citation if your source cites another text. A quote within a quote is called an **embedded quote,** and is formatted as follows:

> The *Mayflower's* passengers were, according to Bradford, "not a little joyful." The clarity of the atmosphere on a crisp autumn day in New England shrinks the distances and accentuates the colors, and the Pilgrims were "much comforted . . . [by] seeing so goodly a land, and wooded to the brink of the sea." Just to make certain, Jones tacked the *Mayflower* and stood in for shore. After an hour or so, all agreed this was indeed Cape Cod. (Philbrick, 2006, p. 35)

To cite an **embedded quote** incorporated into your own writing, use the following format and punctuation:

> Philbrick (2006) details the difficulties of the Atlantic crossing and notes that the *"Mayflower's* passengers were, according to Bradford, 'not a little joyful'" (p. 35).

While it is always preferable to draw from and cite the original source, you may encounter situations in which the original is not readily available or is left uncertain in the source where you found it referenced. Citing one source based on its inclusion in another source is called an "indirect citation." Page-number references for direct quotes must always be included when available, but they may be placed before or after the quote, depending on the position of the parenthetical citation. Clarity is always the governing factor. Here is an example of indirect citation in APA style:

> Boyd and Fales (1983, p. 100) define reflection as the "process of internally examining and exploring an issue of concern, triggered by an experience, which creates and clarifies meaning in terms of self, and which results in a changed conceptual perspective" (as cited in Cranton, 1994, p. 49).

Note: The abbreviation for a single page is (p.), for multiple pages (pp.).

Integrating Sources

Once you've found reliable and pertinent sources, you must integrate the information into your writing. Avoid quoting too much, and think in terms of how a source contributes to your thesis. Use block quotes sparingly, and only when a briefer excerpt is insufficient to illustrate or support your point. Remember that your voice should always direct your essay: if source material makes your argument for you, then it really isn't your argument. You may reference an idea, a text excerpt, a series of pages, a chapter or chapters, or even an entire work in a single citation; however, writing well obligates you to preserve the clarity and continuity of your sources and to remain faithful to the context of the original work when broadly paraphrasing or using ellipses to omit portions of a quote. Be careful to quote accurately, and never omit material to make a quote better fit your argument if the omission will distort or misrepresent the original. How any particular source contributes to the goal of your essay determines the extent to which it should be used and therefore the scope of any given citation. The following examples show a range of ways to cite various types of sources in your writing.

Citing a Work by One Author

This is probably the most common type of citation: it requires only an author's name and a publication year, plus a page number when you quote directly. Previously discussed guidelines apply.

Direct Quote:

> Although, as Rees (2003) declares, "it is a truism that an informed citizenry is essential to a properly functioning democracy," that doesn't necessarily mean that poor test scores on standardized exams are "a sign that our democracy is crumbling" (p. 1).

Paraphrase:

> There is no rational correlation between recent instances of poor standardized test performance among American students and a supposed decline in the state of American democracy (Rees, 2003).

Two or More Works by One Author

In most instances, the year of publication should distinguish among different works by the same author. If a single author has published several sources on the same issue or point of research, they can all be listed within a single parenthetical citation because the dates will differentiate the works in the references list:

> Reflexivity research has a well-established history of examining human cognition in contrast to animal instinct (Mezirow, 1978, 1990, 1991, 1997, 2000).

If you reference two or more works by the same author published in the same year, they should be organized alphabetically by title in the references list and labeled sequentially with the appropriate lowercase letter (a, b, c, etc.). This letter will come immediately after the date in all parenthetical citations, just as it does in the reference list. For example, if you were to use two sources by Hampton published in the same year, *After the Applause Dies* and *Controlling Your Anger,* you would refer to them as "a" and "b," consistent with their alphabetical order in the reference list.

> (Hampton, 2001a)

> (Hampton, 2001b)

In those cases when two authors share the same surname, include the first initial and follow previous rules:

> (L. Alcott, 2002)

> (B. Alcott, 1965)

In some instances you may find that several sources have contributed to your knowledge on a particular topic or issue. In this case, all sources must be acknowledged. This can be most clearly done by incorporating all of them in a single parenthetical citation, separating each full source reference with a semicolon. These multiple source references should be **alphabetized** within the citation according to the surname of the first listed author for each individual source (we've added **bold letters** only for emphasis):

> Research spanning the last 30 years indicates what most of us already suspected, that teacher attitudes and perceptions impact student behavior (**F**ang, 1996; **H**ativa & Goodyear, 2002; **W**illiams, Whitehead, & Miller, 1972).

Works with More than One Author

It is not unusual for scholars to collaborate in the social and behavioral sciences, so you might very well need to incorporate single-source citations that have more than one author. Please don't confuse this with multiple references, which we will discuss next. This can all be a little confusing, so please stay with us through these explanations and examples. When two or more authors are cited parenthetically, the ampersand (&) is used for brevity; when multiple authors are mentioned within the text of the sentence, the word "and" is used to preserve grammatical integrity:

> Recent classification efforts (Miles & Huberman, 1994) have helped us to consolidate much of the disparate work on the implications of Confucian humanism for educational theory.

OR

> Miles and Huberman (1994) helped classify the growing body of work on Confucianism and educational theory.

When a source has only two authors, both are always cited. When there are three, four, or five authors, the first citation should include all of their names in the order they are listed in the source—multiple authors are not always listed in alphabetical order—but subsequent citations can be abbreviated by using the first listed author's last name (surname) followed by the Latin phrase "et al." (which means "and others"). For example, the first time you cite the book *Habits of the Heart*, it would appear this way:

> Bellah, Madsen, Sullivan, Swidler, and Tipton (1985) claim...

Subsequent citations can be abbreviated:

> Bellah et al. (1985) deny that...

For sources with six or more authors, all citations should be abbreviated in this manner: first listed surname followed by "et al." and, as always, publication date.

A Work with No Listed Author (Anonymous)

Apart from anonymously written literary classics, you should show a healthy skepticism of any publication for which no one is willing to take credit. This is doubly true for online works because there are no editors or publishing standards to limit erroneous or false statements. If the author of the text is listed as "Anonymous," use Anonymous as the author's name. Remember that corporations and institutions can also be authors. If you opt to use a source with no listed author, treat the title as the author and follow previous rules, using, as always, the year of publication for the specific source or edition you drew on. A lengthy full title can be shortened to a keyword abbreviation.

An anonymous online example is treated in much the same way, but page numbers are rare for hypertext composed specifically for electronic media. Chapter numbers are a helpful guide for your readers; when they are not available, you must provide either a page number or a paragraph number to locate the citation precisely. Where page breaks are unclear you will need to count paragraphs. The following is a citation for an online source without page or paragraph numbers and with no listed author (the title is shortened from "Dealing with Sudden Infant Death Syndrome"). For this article we had to carefully count the paragraphs to come up with an accurate paragraph location (abbreviated as "para."):

> ("Dealing with Sudden," para. 12)

Here is another example of an online source with no listed author; however, this source has marked paragraph numbers, so no counting was necessary:

> People don't always think only of themselves in times of crisis. One man, for example, had gone out in search of the family cat. Meanwhile, the storm arrived, and "so changed the landscape he got lost" ("Happy Ending," para. 4).

Corporate Author

Citations for corporate authors follow the same general rules outlined so far. The name of the corporation replaces the name of a specific author. Once you have initially identified the group by its full name, you can establish an abbreviation in parentheses and then use the abbreviation for all later citations. Use parentheses the first time to establish the abbreviation but not after that, so that it is not confused with a citation:

The 1999 anthology published by the Science Fiction Research Association (SFRA) concedes that defining the genre is a tricky and uncertain proposition.

The fact that science fiction cannot be easily reduced or pinned down does not mean that it lacks categorical coherence or a clear literary history (SFRA, 1999).

Indirect Sources

While it is always preferable to draw from and cite the original source, you may encounter situations in which the original is not readily available or is left uncertain in the source where you found it referenced. In this situation, your own citation will acknowledge the fact in this way:

(as cited in Cranton, 1994, p. 49)

Dictionaries and Encyclopedias

Most general dictionaries and encyclopedias consist of what is regarded as common knowledge and frequently don't need to be cited. Specialized, discipline-specific dictionaries and encyclopedias, however, should be cited. When it is appropriate to cite from sources arranged alphabetically, as is common with dictionaries and encyclopedias, a page number is not necessary.

Translated Works

In a rare exception to its general rules for citations, APA requires that the citation for a translated work include both the original publication date and that of its translated version:

... (Derrida, 1991/trans. 1992)

Please note that it is the *author* and not the translator who is cited!

Interviews and Personal Communications

Such sources used with good judgment are absolutely legitimate, but interviews and personal communications are considered unpublished or "unrecoverable" sources in APA style. They are not included in your references list, and therefore, they need to be specified in a citation. The date should include the exact day when possible:

(J. Walter, personal communication, April 23, 2007).

The Bible and Other Sacred Texts

Because of their special status and prominence, sacred texts from well-established religious traditions represent a special case when it comes to citations, and their titles are rarely indicated in the same way as the titles of other published texts. Books of the Bible should be abbreviated and then, without additional punctuation, followed by specific reference to chapter and verse (line), with a colon separating chapter from verse. The first time you cite it, include the specific translation as well:

...Gen. 1:23 (New Jerusalem Bible)

Once you have established the translation or edition of the Bible you will be citing (an accepted standard such as *The King James, The New Jerusalem,* or *The New International Version*), the title information can be excluded from subsequent citations, as long as you continue to use that same version:

(Rev. 11:3–13)

Note: No additional reference is necessary for the Bible beyond an in-text citation. This is a rare exception: do not include it in your reference list.

Tables and Illustrations

When a table, graph, illustration, or other figure is inserted into an essay, the full bibliographic reference for the source should be listed directly below it. Here is a typical example, but if you are writing for publication, you will need to master the more complex rules for incorporating tables, graphs, and figures as source material in your research writing.

Table 1

Proportion of Free Negroes, Whites, and Slaves Urban* 1860

	Free Negroes	Whites	Slaves
United States	62.5%	51.2%	--
North	55.7%	48.5%	--
South	72.7%	68.7%	46.8%
Upper South	69.2%	69.4%	41.8%
Lower South	85.5%	66.7%	51.4%

*All places incorporated and unincorporated, greater than 2,500 in population.

Source: *Population of the United States in 1860.* (1864). Washington, DC.

Oral and Electronic Presentations

If you read a paper aloud or deliver an oral presentation that draws on outside sources, you must cite the sources of information for direct and paraphrased material aloud as well. Most presenters dispense with page numbers when giving source information orally, and they make it verbally clear when they are citing another source. One way to do this is to introduce the author's name and publication date, and say aloud "quote" and "unquote" (or "end quote") to begin and end quoted material. Some people prefer to make the "air quote" sign (both hands up in a sort of modified peace sign, they waggle their fingers to begin and end the quotation). If the material is paraphrased, you can simply say something like: "according to…" or "as _____ claims." Some adept presenters can make clear the beginning and end of their source material just by vocal intonation, though it is probably best to err on the side of being explicit. Create a references page for a paper to be read aloud just as you would for a written essay.

When using print images (charts, pictures, maps, etc.), you should attach the source information to the image (or near it in cases where it might damage the document). It is also a good idea to identify the source aloud if it might be difficult for the audience to read from afar.

As with a paper that is read aloud, an electronic presentation should include a references page. The references page should be included in the electronic presentation, but it is a good idea to bring at least one paper copy along. For electronic presentations, you may cite images and text parenthetically just as you would in a print essay. Various software programs such as PowerPoint® give you a variety of ways to overlay text on, above, or below images. If your citation is clearly readable on or attached to the image, you do not need to read it aloud. For an example of how to cite an online image or movie, see the Electronic Sources section of this guide.

Footnotes and Endnotes

APA style permits the inclusion of either endnotes[1] or footnotes[2] to provide additional information for your readers or to elaborate on sources not directly pertinent to your own discussion. Both types of notes are provided as conveniences and courtesies for your readers: use them sparingly, as information vital to your project should be presented and cited within the main text.

Endnotes

[1]Endnotes appear in this format, on a page with the word "Endnotes" centered at the top. The page should appear after the text of the essay itself and the "References" page. Endnotes should be double-spaced.

---

[2]Footnotes fall at the bottom of the page, in this format, and provide information or references indirectly related to the focus of your discussion and research. They are double-spaced.

4

Sample Student Paper with References Page

Running head: POCAHONTAS   1

Pocahontas: Less than Her Myth, More than a Myth

Janie Evans

October 7, 2007

continued

↑1 inch
POCAHONTAS   ↓1/2 inch
                                                    2

Janie Evans

Professor Gonzales

Humanities 107

October 7, 2007

       Pocahontas: Less than Her Myth, More than a Myth

    ⟶ Many people have at least some familiarity with the
1/2 inch
mythical name Pocahontas before being introduced to the

story of Jamestown when they learn about U.S. history. Disney

Studios' controversial adaptation of the story of the young Indian

"princess" and her fight to save the English adventurer Captain

John Smith offers just one of many popular culture depictions

of this widely known but often misunderstood Native American

⟵→figure. We seem to want her part in our American mythology to be⟵→
1 inch
that of the romantic heroine—beautiful, brave, honorable, and   1 inch

devoted to her new love from across the seas. Such images and

expectations rely on severe distortions of situations and events,

yet Pocahontas did play an extremely significant role in colonial

history. She is an American hero because of the fact that she

contributed to the survival of the Jamestown settlers and was a

crucial force in easing the potentially explosive tensions between

the English colonists in Virginia and the confederation of native

nations headed by her father, Powhatan. Simultaneously, though,

Pocahontas symbolizes the tragic consequences of European

colonization, whose impact obliterated traditional societies and

culture even when native peoples were able to survive and adapt.
    ↑1 inch
    ↓

(Proportions shown in this paper are adjusted to fit space limitations of this book. Follow
actual dimensions discussed in this book and your instructor's directions.)

POCAHONTAS   3

  Pocahontas was born in c. 1596 as Matoaka to her clan and Amonte to her parents; the nickname of Pocahontas has been translated as "playful one," but it has less positive associations in Algonquian usage, meaning "spoiled" or "naughty child" (Crazy Horse, 2003). A favorite of her father, Chief Powhatan, she was by most accounts a vibrant personality who made a strong impression on all of the Jamestown colonists, including John Smith. Smith very nearly met with execution for insubordination on the trip over in 1607 at the hands of his own countrymen and was saved only by a set of sealed orders from the governing council in London naming him among the leaders of the new colony. This same arrogant, rowdy John Smith is the sole source for the first and most compelling episode in Pocahontas' myth.[1] The lone survivor of an ambushed hunting party, Smith (2003) reports that after several days in captivity he was brought before Powhatan, who ordered that he be put to death, but that fate, this time in the form of Pocahontas, once more came to his rescue:

   [T]wo great stones were brought before Powhatan; then as

   many as could, laid hands on him, dragged him to them,

   and thereon laid his head and being ready with their clubs

---

[1]Smith never mentions Pocahontas in any of his writings prior to her death in 1617. This fact has been mentioned frequently in any number of analyses of the events reported. The general trend of many of these is to suggest that Smith invented, or at least embroidered the story, as part of a campaign of promotional propaganda to encourage colonization.

continued

to beat out his brains, Pocahontas, the King's dearest daughter, when no entreaty could prevail, got his head in her arms and laid her own upon his to save him from death, whereat the Emperor [still referring to Powhatan] was contented...(p. 51)

Pocahontas believed that the Indians had things to learn from the English (Gili, 1995).

Allen (2003) and Baym et al. (2003) question whether or not Smith's life was actually in danger, as he reports it, or whether he misconstrued a ritualistic pageant, yet Pocahontas may have intervened at another point by necessity: there is some evidence that she acted as "an informer for the colony, warning Smith of her father's belligerent plans" when Powhatan threatened Smith's life in 1608 (Board of Supervisors, 2002). At the very least it seems clear that Pocahontas established an early pattern of intervening on behalf of Smith and the English colonists.

Like so many other early colonies, Jamestown was beset with troubles of every kind, and like every other previous English colony, it came very near to complete collapse. Pocahontas was prominent among those who directly helped the colonists avoid starvation. Tradition holds that she and Smith remained on friendly terms—though nothing indicates intimate relations between them—but there are no other details of direct interactions between Pocahontas and Smith in America prior to her own visit to England in 1616; Smith himself returned

POCAHONTAS   5

in 1609.[2] Pocahontas disappears from the historical records
entirely until 1613, when she was kidnapped by the Jamestown
colonists (having been lured aboard a ship in the Potomac by
two of her own people in exchange for manufactured goods,
if accounts are valid) and used as a political tool against
Powhatan. She does not appear to have been directly abused or
mistreated, but she was held for an extended length of time.
During this captivity, Pocahontas converted to Christianity, in
contrast to the ideal depicted by Disney in 1995, which glorifies
the persistence of native spirituality: "O Great Spirit, hear our
song / Help us keep the ancient ways / Keep the sacred fire
strong/Walk in balance all our days" (Schwartz, 1995, lines
13–16). She is believed to be the first Native American to so
convert, and she was baptized with the given name of Rebecca.

One of the colonists, John Rolfe, who was a widower, took
a "special interest" in Pocahontas, and they were married in
1614 with the apparent blessings of Powhatan and the governor
of Virginia (as cited in Crazy Horse, 2003). Some historians remain
suspicious of Rolfe's motives since tobacco profits were involved,
but a relative peace did follow between Powhatan's people and
the colonists for the next several years. Rolfe and Rebecca nee

---

[2]They did, however, meet again in London, when she visited with husband
John Rolfe in 1616. Smith claims that the meeting was cordial. Other
evidence indicates some ill will toward Smith on Pocahontas' part
(Crazy Horse).

continued

POCAHONTAS   6

Pocahontas had a son, Thomas, in 1615, and in 1616 the Virginia

Company encouraged the family to visit England. Upon their

arrival, Pocahontas was presented to King James I and Queen

Anne, along with many other high-society members. She was

deemed a princess, "a European misconception about Indian

society that persists to this day" (Virginia Historical Society,

2003). She is rumored to have captivated poet and playwright

Ben Jonson (Ross, 1999), and it was during this stay that the

famous Simon van de Passe engraving was done—the only such

portrait in existence (Virginia Historical Society, 2003). All of

this served to enhance and strengthen the emerging myth.

Then in 1617, at the young age of 22, just when her family

was to return to Virginia, Pocahontas became very ill and died

suddenly, probably of a commonplace European illness against

which she lacked resistance. It is actually uncertain how she died;

some historians say she died of smallpox, others say tuberculosis

or pneumonia. She was buried in Gravesend, England. John Rolfe

would return to Virginia alone, leaving Thomas to be raised and

educated by his family in England. Powhatan himself died the

next spring. Without Pocahontas' presence and efforts, the always

uneasy relations in Virginia eroded over the next several years,

and eventually degenerated into destructive warfare.

The story of Pocahontas has been called a myth, and

most of us expect the key figure in a myth to be a hero, who, as

Mossiker (1976, p. 11) states, has "relevance to their origins,

survival, development, happiness or glory." She can be called a

POCAHONTAS   7

hero because she helped keep the Virginia colony afloat and establish the first successful English outpost in America. As a result, more colonists were inspired to take the adventure across the Atlantic to a "New World." Speaking on behalf of the contemporary Powhatan Nation, however, Chief Roy Crazy Horse (2003) states that the mythical figure popularized by Disney is "the hero of Euro-Americans . . . [,] the 'good Indian'" used to help justify historical abuses against Native American rights.

Pocahontas herself has no say in the myth. Historians and special interests have pieced together her tale from scant documentation and Smith's questionable *General History* in support of their own agendas. The subsequent pictorial history—marked by a progressive softening, whitening, and, finally, abandoning of the native features captured by Van de Passe—perhaps most clearly demonstrates this (Board of Supervisors, 2002). Regardless of how Pocahontas' contributions are perceived, for a woman—particularly such a youthful woman—to have had such an impact on our history is amazing in an otherwise male-dominated arena. Pocahontas at the age of 12 was giving advice to her father, acting as a liaison between dramatically different cultures, and perhaps even serving as a spy for either or both sides. She is both more and less than the popular myth. She will remain simultaneously an icon of America's success and a tragic reminder of the cost at which it came.

POCAHONTAS   8

References

Allen, P. G. (2003). *Pocahontas*. San Francisco, CA: Harper.

Baym, N. et al. (Ed.). (2003). Introduction to John Smith. *The
      Norton anthology of American literature* (shorter 6th ed.,
      pp. 42–44). New York, NY: Norton.

Board of Supervisors and County Manager's Office Henrico County,
      Virginia. (2002). *The four faces of Pocahontas*. Retrieved
      April 24, 2007, from http://www.co.henrico.va.us

Crazy Horse, Chief Roy. (2003, May). The Pocahontas myth.
      Campfire stories. Retrieved April 22, 2007 from
      Manataka American Indian Council web site:
      http://www.manataka.org

Gili, J. (Writer/Director). (1995). *Pocahontas, her true story*
      [Motion picture]. Britain: Worldwide Americans.

Mossiker, F. (1976). *Pocahontas*. New York, NY: Knopf.

Ross, J. F. (1999, January). Picturing Pocahontas.
      Smithsonian, 34–36.

Smith, J. (2003). *General history of Virginia, New England, and
      the Summer Isles*. In N. Baym et al. (Eds.), *The Norton
      anthology of American literature* (shorter 6th ed.,
      pp. 44–53). New York, NY: Norton.

Schwartz, S. (1995). Steady as the beating drum. *Pocahontas*
      [Motion picture]. Gabriel, M., & Goldman, E. (Directors).
      United States: Walt Disney Studios.

Virginia Historical Society. *The story of Virginia: Contact and
      conflict*. Retrieved from http://www.vahistorical.org

5

Creating a References Page

APA

Key Terms

Archival Version The final version of any source, regardless of medium or format. An online book scanned from a print source, a journal article stored in a database, and a newspaper article in the final edition of the paper are all archival versions. When referencing an archival copy, no date of retrieval is needed because the source is assumed to be in its permanent form.

Author The writer/creator/originator of a source. There may be a single author, multiple authors, or a corporate entity listed as the author. The author is the identifier for a source, both in text and in the references section—indeed, the word "authority" is derived from "author." Works with no listed author, particularly **secondary sources,** should be used sparingly and with skepticism.

Bibliography A list of key sources relating to a particular subject or area of research. It differs from a list of references in that it goes beyond the sources cited within a particular piece of scholarship to provide a broad list of the sources used or consulted during the research process. Most bibliographies are labeled "Selective Bibliography" because few can claim to be a complete list of all pertinent sources. An "Annotated Bibliography" provides a brief description (or abstract) of each listed source.

Edition A particular version of a source; multiple editions indicate either periodic updates, as with many standardized textbooks, or a varied publication history, as is often the case with public domain (originally published prior to the emergence of modern copyright laws) literary texts. If no edition or editorial information appears on a title page, you can assume that the source is a first edition or a reprint thereof. However, if you were to cite a modern edition of Charles Brockden Brown's 1798 novel *Wieland* in an essay, you'd likely find that it has an editor, an introduction, and possibly even an afterword (such editorial supplements are cited differently from how the text itself is cited: please see our examples of reference listings). If a text has been updated, revised, or abridged, that will be reflected in its edition designation: for example, 3rd ed., Rev. ed., Abr. ed.

Electronic Media   All publications, databases, postings, and sources that are accessed for academic use in Internet or hypertext format. (Print material is referred to as "fixed media".) Obviously, this includes a diverse range of material, and APA provides reference examples for citing web sources such as journal articles, electronic books, bibliographies, raw data, etc. The following terms are useful when dealing with electronic sources.

> **Database** A collection of electronically stored information. Many databases allow access only through paid subscriptions, generally purchased by your campus library and available through its catalog. For a list of available databases and their merits, see Chapter 2.

> **DOI (Digital Object Identifier)** A unique string of letters and numbers that identifies a specific online document and provides a link to its content. When a DOI is available (it may be hidden under a "button"), it must be included in a journal article reference. Like URLs, DOIs can be long, so it is often best to cut and paste the alphanumeric string to avoid retyping errors.

> **URL (Uniform Resource Locator)** This is the address that appears when you access a web site; it contains valuable information for determining the source's origins and credibility. See Chapter 2 for a discussion of how to read URLs.

Periodical (and Nonperiodical)   Most newspapers, magazines, and journals are called periodicals because they are published at regular intervals (daily, weekly, monthly, quarterly, etc.). Nonperiodicals are works such as books, pamphlets, and many web sources such as home pages, digitized print material, and online postings.

Primary and Secondary Source   A **primary source** is a direct item of evidence pertaining to the subject under discussion, or, in the case of literary or artistic criticism, it is the actual text being critiqued. Other examples of primary sources include information from an experiment you conducted, data from a survey you administered, and (in most cases) a historical document you retrieved from an archive. A **secondary source** presents external, after-the-fact commentary, research, or analysis relevant to your research topic and particular position. Secondary sources will generally make up the bulk of the sources undergraduates use because they provide access to the expertise of professionals in any given field and allow you to benefit from the sum total of previous research in the particular area. For example, in an essay about the function of carved figurines in Neolithic belief systems, the figurines themselves, cave drawings used for comparison, and parallels from more recent tribal art would all be primary sources; an interpretive article by Maria Gimbutas on the subject would be a secondary source. When you write a research paper for a college course, you add a secondary source to the pool of resources available in the world of information.

Publisher   The agency, entity, or person sponsoring the production and circulation of (usually) written materials. Such alternative media as film and music have terminology and distribution channels distinct to those industries, but the parallel remains valid. Publication "presses" might reside within a reputable university, lending their publications additional credibility, or they might operate in the private sector as trade publishers, where profit is the driving force and *caveat emptor* ("let the buyer beware") is the rule. In the case of newspapers and other periodicals, the name of the publisher is that of the publication itself, such as *The New York Times,* so no additional publisher need be indicated in your reference list. Be leery of self-published materials or web-based publications lacking affiliation or substantiation (see the Evaluating Print Sources section in Chapter 2).

Scholarly Journal (and Peer Review)   Scholarly journals are carefully edited for verifiable content, proper attribution and use of sources, and significance within their respective fields. They are generally published quarterly (or less frequently), and they contain articles by professionals and experts. They are also generally "peer reviewed," which means that other experts read and comment on the submissions before they are accepted for publication. The high level of professionalism, article selection, and editing make scholarly journals excellent secondary sources.

Volume and Issue   Scholarly journals often consider one year's worth of publications a "volume," and each "issue" of the journal a part of that volume. For this reason, scholarly journals frequently use continuous pagination throughout each volume—for example, if issue 1 ends on page 136, issue 2 will begin on page 137.

The References Page

A research essay in the APA style concludes with a list that includes every source cited in the body of the paper. As the term *references* indicates, only the works referenced during your discussion are included here, and each in-text citation in your essay must correspond to an entry in your reference list.

Alphabetize the reference list so that your reader can match a source citation within your essay to the complete publishing information for that source. Alphabetize sources by the last name of each author (use the name of the first author listed when there are more than one); by the first substantive word (excluding articles "The" "An," and "A") in a corporate author's name; or by the first substantive word of the source's title when no author's name is provided.

Please let us emphasize this general rule once more: *Every source listed in your references page must concur with a citation within the body of your essay.* The few exceptions to this rule appear on pages 57. This rule distinguishes a

references section from a **bibliography**—a listing of all sources consulted pertinent to your research.

Your references section should be formatted as follows (see the references list on page 40):

- It should stand alone as the last section of your research paper, separate from the main text, tables, graphs, or illustrations. It should be titled "References," centered at the top of the page, and the first entry should begin one double-spaced increment below the title.
- Individual entries should be alphabetized according to each author's last name or the first substantive word of the title when no author is listed.
- Each alphabetized entry should begin with the first line at the left margin and subsequent lines indented five spaces. This reversal of standard indentation allows authors' names to stand out for easy reading.
- The entire section should be double-spaced, with no additional space between entries.

Keep in mind that the majority of your information will be derived from credible print sources, and a typical book entry, therefore, will require the following:

> Author's Last Name, Initial(s). (Year of publication). *Full and italicized title of the work*. City or Other Place of Publication: Name of Publisher.

Note that only the first word of a title and proper names are capitalized. Also capitalize the first word after a colon in a title.

There are a variety of exceptions and additions to this format. The following examples are designed to cover the sources you will most frequently use and cite in your research writing. Internet sources, probably the most familiar to students, can offer significant challenges in terms of citation. (Chapter 2 offers advice on how to find and evaluate a variety of sources.)

Electronic Sources

The Internet (Web)

It has been said that you can never step into the same river twice, and the same is true of the Internet. It is a constantly changing venue where information is transitory and can disappear without notice. Even when information endures, it may appear on different sites in different stages of update and with different links. There are thus fewer standards for citing publication information from web sites than there are for print sources, and this can lead to problems in identifying sources clearly. Furthermore, electronic forms are always evolving, making a standard way of citing them difficult to establish. In many ways the web represents the "Wild West" of research sources; nonetheless, the most common entries will take one of the following forms:

> Author's Last Name, Initial. (Date). *Title of document*. *Publication Name*. DOI

> Author's Last Name, Initial. (Date). *Title of document*. *Publication Name*. Retrieved from URL

Because electronic publications are less durable than print sources, you need to give additional information when citing them. In cases where the content of the document is subject to change, you should provide the date you retrieved the data. When a source is in its final, or archival, state, no retrieval date is necessary. You should, however, provide a web address for *all* sources, preferably a DOI (Digital Object Identifier). A DOI provides a persistent link to a document's location on the Internet regardless of any modifications, and therefore it is a more reliable identifier than a URL. If no DOI is available, you will need to supply a URL (Uniform Resource Locater). Check the URL before submitting your paper—if it doesn't work, remove the source from your paper. If the URL is excessively long or is available by subscription only, specify the URL for the home, menu, or catalog page (you may have to "undo" the automatic formatting that some word processing programs impose in order to change the URL format to fit properly in your references page). Give the URL for the home or menu page for online dictionaries and encyclopedias, or for material presented in independent frames.

You will not always be able to find all the citation information that APA calls for with every online source you consult, but look over the site carefully to find all the information that is available. When there is no author, publisher, or sponsor listed at all, you should not rely on the source. The following examples are meant to serve as a guide to citing electronic publications, but be aware that citation standards will continue to change as technology does. A final reminder: **include a URL only if there is no DOI.**

Online Journal Article with No DOI

The following example is from a journal that has no print counterpart, has no DOI, and exists only online; therefore, it is essential to include a working URL in your citation. Because this is the archival copy (final version), no retrieval date is required.

> Tietje, L. (2005, June). Hegemonic visualism. *Radical Pedagogy*. Retrieved from http://radicalpedagogy
> .icaap.org/

Journal Article with DOI

Although the following source was retrieved from the PsycInfo database, neither the database nor the URL need be listed in the citation because the DOI serves as a reliable identifier of the content and functions as a link to the source. The DOI, therefore, takes the place of both the database name and the URL in your citation. Because this is an archival copy, no retrieval date is required.

Print Journal Accessed Online with No DOI

Because this article is from an archived copy of a print journal, you do not need to give the retrieval date (See "When to Use a Retrieval Date" below). Because there is no DOI, a URL is required.

> Terror comes to London. (2005, August 1). *The Nation, 3*. Retrieved from http://www.thenation.com/
> doc/20050801/editors

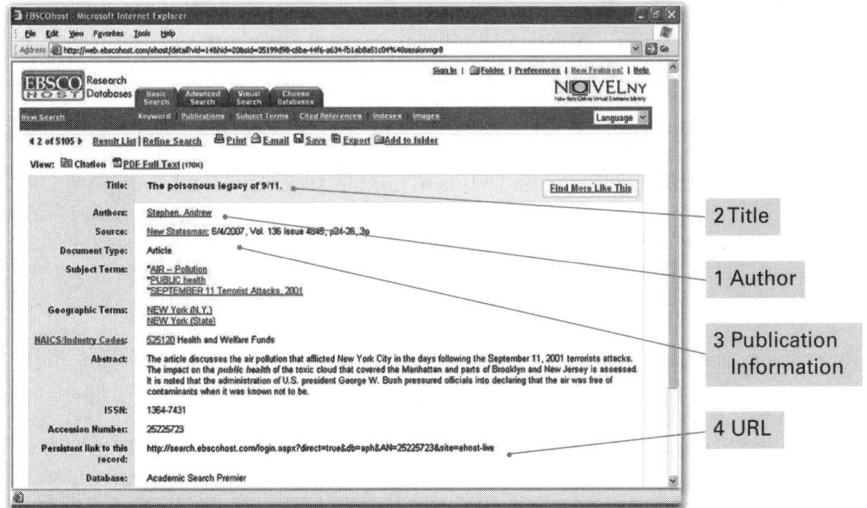

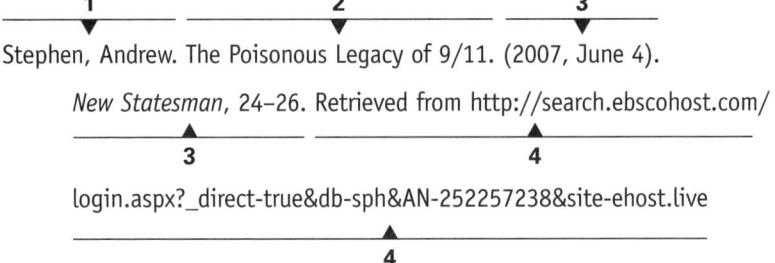

A Newspaper Article Online

Print versions and electronic versions of the same newspaper often contain different information, so an article accessed from an electronic version of a newspaper should be cited as an electronic source, with a URL.

Herbert, R. (2006, January 19). Who will stand up for the Constitution? *The New York Times*. Retrieved from http://select.nytimes.com

An Article from a Database (Library Subscription Service)

In the interest of simplifying the reference format, APA style no longer requires the inclusion of a database name. You may include it as a courtesy if the source is particularly difficult to find, but as a general rule you should leave it out. Different databases use different filing systems, and they will sometimes offer an "accession number," a "document number," or an "item number." For extremely hard-to-locate documents, these numbers can help a researcher track down an obscure source, so you may add the number at the end of the citation in parentheses as a courtesy to your readers. **Do not include a database name for most reference entries.** It is never used when a DOI is available.

> Ware, E. A., Uttal, D. H., Wetter, E. K., & DeLoache, J. S. (2006). Young children make scale errors when playing with dolls. *Developmental Science, 9*(1), 40–45. Retrieved from Psychology and Behavioral Sciences Collection database. (19149472)

When to Use a Retrieval Date

As you may have noticed, none of the examples we've provided so far includes a retrieval date. An APA reference requires a retrieval date only when there is no fixed publication date for the source, or for content on the web that may change at any time. The archival versions listed above are not likely to change, but many web sites are subject to updates, additions, or even deletion. You might find yourself citing an unfinished dissertation, a study still in preparation, or a preprint of a journal article. Because all of these examples are likely to be changed or updated, it is important to include the date you accessed the data. The following two examples show how to include a retrieval date in your reference.

Web Page or Nonperiodical Web Document

Internet sites are notorious for not providing, or making it difficult to find, citation information. But you need to locate as much citation information as you can. If you cannot find a publication date, use "n.d." (for "no date") where the date is usually listed. If you find a web site with no listed author or date (a common occurrence when researching on the web) you should consider carefully its value and credibility as a source. Don't forget, however, that institutions and organizations can also be considered authors. Both sources below are derived from academic web sites that undergo occasional updates.

> Campbell, D. (2005, July 18). *Naturalism in American literature.* Retrieved August 5, 2005, from http://www.wsu.edu/~campbell/amlit/natural.htm
>
> London, J. G. (2006, July 25). A short biography of Jack London. *The Jack London online collection.* Retrieved September 18, 2008, from http://london.sonoma.edu/jackbio.html

Online Encyclopedias and Dictionaries

The content of general dictionaries and encyclopedias is often considered common knowledge (see the Key Terms list in Chapter 3) and thus may not need to be cited. Specialized and discipline-specific reference sources (such as *Stanford's*

Online Encyclopedia of Philosophy or the example below), however, should be cited. Do not rely on the authority of wiki reference sources; anyone may contribute to and edit them, and this cannot help but make them of questionable reliability. Individual entries in encyclopedias and dictionaries often do not list an author or a date, and the date of the most recent revision is not always clear. When no author is given, begin the reference entry with the title, or the term being defined, and use "(n.d.)" if there is no clear date for the entry. Whenever there is no listed posting or revision date, be sure to include a retrieval date.

> Acculturation. (n.d.). *Encyclopedia of psychology*. Retrieved September 19, 2008, from
> http://www.archive.org/details/HabiPat1954

Online Bibliography

Whether it comes from an open web site, courseware, or an online book, be sure to clearly label the source. You may also need to identify the source as "[Bibliography]" directly after the title if that is not clear from the title.

> Byrne, A., & Hilbert, D. (n.d.). *A bibliography of color and philosophy*. Retrieved October 1, 2008,
> from Massachusetts Institute of Technology Philosophy web site: http://web.mit.edu/
> philos/www/color-biblio.html

Weblog (Blog) Post

For both blog postings and electronic mailing lists, use "Message posted to" and then the name of the site to which the message was posted:

> Martin, G. (2008, September 9). News from HBO. Message posted to http://grrm.livejournal.com/

Online Image

The creator is listed first, followed by publication date, title, and description of the medium in brackets, for example, "[Painting]" or "[Collage]." Although the image cited in the following example is archived and therefore not likely to change, when no date is given for an online image or for the web site where it resides, you should provide a retrieval date and a URL.

> Royal Astronomical Society. (n.d.). *Newton's reflector telescope* [Photograph]. Retrieved January
> 27, 2009, from Amazing Space web site: http://www.amazingspace.stsci.edu

Online Video

List the producer, director, or creator first. Online moving images can range from home videos to flash animation to commerical films. The broad range of possibilities may require you to improvise a bit for certain sources. Here are two examples for citing online videos:

> Knickerbocker Productions. (Producer). (1954). *Habit patterns* [Motion picture]. In McGraw Hill,
> *Psychology for living series*. Retrieved from http://www.archive.org/details/HabiPat1954

> Spiridellis, G., & Spiridellis, E. (Producers/Directors). (2008, July). *Time for some campaignin'*
> [Flash animation]. JibJab Media. Retrieved from http://sendables.jibjab.com

Note: To designate nonverbal media, you use square brackets, an otherwise rare formatting convention in APA style.

E-mail

Personal interviews, telephone conversations, e-mail, letters, etc., are not considered "recoverable data" in the APA style (because they are not professionally archived); therefore, they are not listed in the references section. See page 29 for an example of how to cite an e-mail in your text.

CD-ROM

Though CD-ROMs were quite popular several years ago, publishers are now issuing fewer and fewer of them periodically, in favor of online databases—another example of the evolving nature of electronic sources.

Troy, L. (2003). Ship and boat building. *Almanac of Business and Industrial Financial Ratios 34*, 157–158. [CD-ROM]. Aspen Publishing.

Print Periodicals

Not too surprisingly, these are texts that are published periodically, generally on a set time schedule (daily, weekly, monthly, quarterly, etc.). Newspapers, magazines, and journals (scholarly, trade, opinion, etc.) are all periodicals. Periodicals require more specific date information than do books, down to the day in the case of most newspapers. (Online periodicals are covered in "Electronic Sources," page 44).

Newspaper Articles

Some newspapers, such as *USA Today* and *The New York Times,* appear in different editions in different parts of the country. These editions are usually indicated at the top of page 1 on the masthead: "national ed.," "late ed.," "western ed.," "overseas ed.," etc. Such special edition information can be listed in parentheses after the title: "(Overseas ed.)." If the article appears on just one page, use "p." for "page," but if it is spread over more than one page, use "pp." for "pages." If the article is not on sequential pages—for example, if it starts on page A1 and continues on page A9—use a comma to separate the pages: "pp. A1, A9."

Semple, K. (2005, July 18). Iraqis stunned by the violence of a bombing. *The New York Times* (National. ed.), pp. A1, A11.

Letter to the Editor

Davidson, M. (2006, January 8). Police state is upon us [Letter to the editor]. *The Spokesman Review,* p. B7.

A Book Review in a Newspaper

Donahue, D. (2005, August 2). [Review of the book *The lady and the panda*]. *USA Today,* p. D5.

Popular Magazines

If the publication gives a volume number, list that number (in italics) directly after the publication title. Unlike newspaper citations, magazine and journal citations do not use "pp." for pages, but simply list the numbers after the volume number. In the example below, the article is in volume 376, begins on page 13, and is continued on page 31. For book reviews and letters to the editor, follow the format of the newspaper examples, using brackets, as in the motion picture review below. Brackets are used for description and are not part of the title.

Weekly Magazine Article with No Listed Author

America's unhappy borders. (2005, August 27). *The Economist, 376,* 13, 31.

Motion Picture Review in a Magazine

Corliss, R. (2006, January 9). [Review of the motion picture *The march of the penguins*]. *Time, 167,* 61.

Scholarly Journals

Scholarly journals are aimed at professionals and students in a specific field and tend to be more serious in tone and subject matter than popular magazines. They are generally edited and refereed by people who have risen to the top of their professions and are considered strong research sources. Some journals may have only a volume number while others will also have an issue number; In APA style you need to cite an issue number only when the journal is separately paginated in each issue (i.e., each issue begins on page 1).

Continuous Pagination by Volume

Many journals start with page 1 at the beginning of their publishing year and continuously number the pages of each issue until the final page of the last issue of the year. For this reason you may find an issue that begins on page 345 and ends on page 460. Do not include the issue number of a continuously paginated volume. The volume number is listed *in italics* following the title. If a journal does not use volume numbers, include the month in the date.

Separate Pagination by Issue

When each new issue begins with page 1, include the **issue number in parentheses but not in italics** directly after the volume number (with no space between the volume and issue numbers).

Ware, E. A., Uttal, D. H., Wetter, E. K., & DeLoache, J. S. (2006). Young children make scale errors when playing with dolls. *Developmental Science, 9*(1), 40–45.

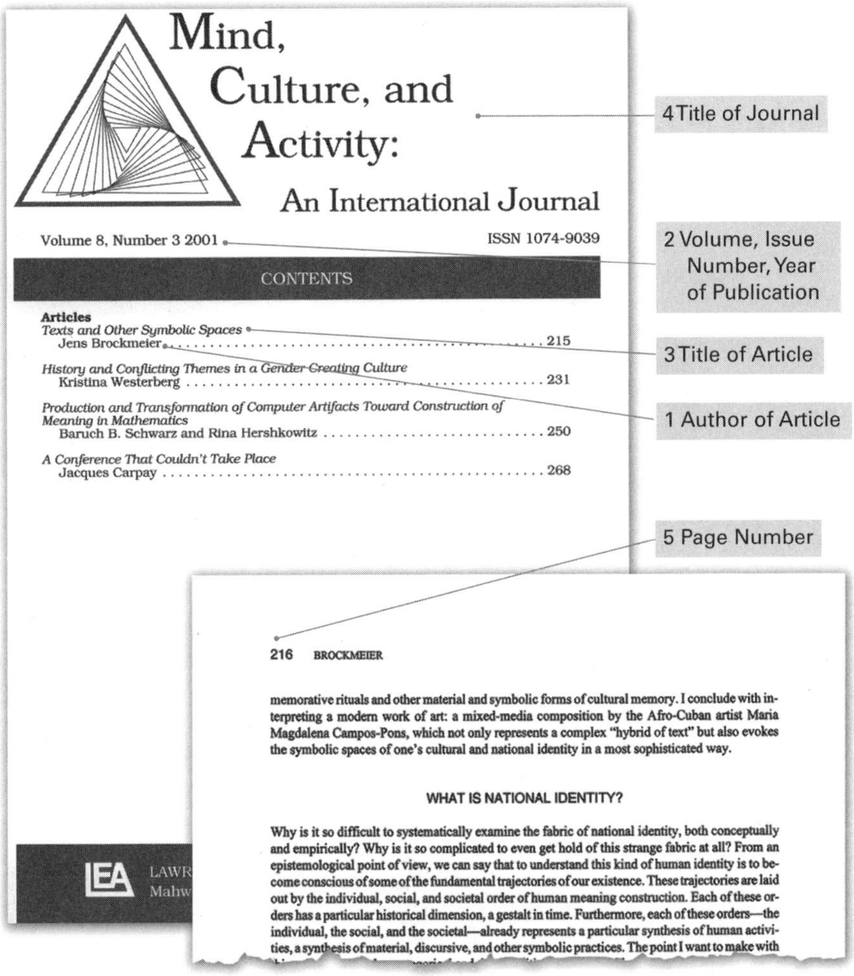

Mind,
Culture, and
Activity:
An International Journal

Volume 8, Number 3 2001   ISSN 1074-9039

CONTENTS

Articles

4 Title of Journal

2 Volume, Issue Number, Year of Publication

3 Title of Article

1 Author of Article

5 Page Number

216   BROCKMEIER

memorative rituals and other material and symbolic forms of cultural memory. I conclude with interpreting a modern work of art: a mixed-media composition by the Afro-Cuban artist Maria Magdalena Campos-Pons, which not only represents a complex "hybrid of text" but also evokes the symbolic spaces of one's cultural and national identity in a most sophisticated way.

WHAT IS NATIONAL IDENTITY?

Why is it so difficult to systematically examine the fabric of national identity, both conceptually and empirically? Why is it so complicated to even get hold of this strange fabric at all? From an epistemological point of view, we can say that to understand this kind of human identity is to become conscious of some of the fundamental trajectories of our existence. These trajectories are laid out by the individual, social, and societal order of human meaning construction. Each of these orders has a particular historical dimension, a gestalt in time. Furthermore, each of these orders—the individual, the social, and the societal—already represents a particular synthesis of human activities, a synthesis of material, discursive, and other symbolic practices. The point I want to make with

LEA   LAWR
    Mahw

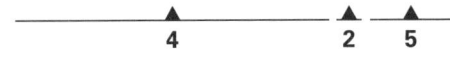

```
         1          2                    3                      4
```

Brockmeier, J. (2001). Texts and other symbolic spaces. *Mind, Culture, and*

    Activity: An International Journal, 8, 215–230.

```
                    4                    2    5
```

Books

Books with a single author generally follow the formula shown above. Your information should be drawn from the **title page,** not from the cover of the book. Note that only the first word, proper nouns, and the first word after a colon are capitalized in a title.

FREAKONOMICS

A ROGUE ECONOMIST EXPLORES
THE HIDDEN SIDE OF EVERYTHING

"Prepare to be dazzled."
— Malcolm Gladwell, author of *The Tipping Point* and *Blink*

NEW YORK
TIMES
BESTSELLER

STEVEN D. LI
STEPHEN J.

FREAKONOMICS

A Rogue Economist

Explores the Hidden

Side of Everything

Steven D. Levitt
and
Stephen J. Dubner

William Morrow
An Imprint of HarperCollins*Publishers*

3 Title

4 Subtitle

1 Authors

6 Publisher

2 Date of Publication

FREAKONOMICS. Copyright © 2005 by Steven D. Levitt and Stephen J. Dubner.
All rights reserved. Printed in the United States of America. No part of this book may be used
or reproduced in any manner whatsoever without written permission except in the case of brief
quotations embodied in critical articles and reviews. For information address HarperCollins
Publishers Inc., 10 East 53rd Street, New York, NY 10022.

HarperCollins books may be purchased for educational, business, or sales promotional use.
For information please write: Special Markets Department, HarperCollins Publishers Inc.,
10 East 53rd Street, New York, NY 10022.

FIRST EDITION

5 Place of Publication

Levitt, S. D., & Dubner, S. J. (2005). *Freakonomics: A rogue economist explores the hidden side of everything.* New York, NY: William Morrow-HarperCollins.

Book with One Author

Phares, V. (1999). *Poppa psychology: The role of fathers in children's well-being.* Westport, CT: Praeger.

Book with Two Authors

Levitt, S. D., & Dubner, S. J. (2005). *Freakonomics: A rogue economist explores the hidden side of everything.* New York, NY: William Morrow-Harper.

Book with up to Six Authors

In this example Bellah is both an author and the editor of the work.

Bellah, R. N. (Ed.), Madsen, R., Sullivan, W. M., Swidler, A., & Tipton, S. M. (1985). *Habits of the heart: Individualism and commitment in American life.* New York, NY: Harper and Row.

Book with Seven or More Authors

For the sake of space, APA style allows for the abbreviation of a group of seven or more authors. Following the name of the sixth listed author, "et al." (meaning "and others") is used. Be aware of the distinction between authors, translators, and editors, especially when dealing with anthologies.

A Translated Book and Tricky Names

Surnames (last names) preceded by articles or prepositions (such as "de," "von," "la," "du," etc.) are generally alphabetized by the surname rather than the article. "Saint" (abbreviated "St.") is considered part of the surname and should be alphabetized accordingly, while "Junior" (abbreviated "Jr.") is treated like an article, and is not used to alphabetize the name.

> St. Mery, M. de. (1947). *Moreau de St. Mery's American journey* (K. Roberts & A. M. Roberts, Trans.). New York, NY: Doubleday.

A Chapter or an Article in an Edited Book

Your references entry for an edited collection or text will depend on how you are using it. If you refer to a work within an edited collection, begin your entry with the author's name (last name, then initials, and alphabetized accordingly) and year of publication followed by the title of the chapter or article; then write "In" followed by the editors' names (here the editors' initials precede the last name), the title of the collection, and the pages of the chapter or article.

> Balter, L. (1999). Metacognitive development. In L. Balter & C. S. Tamis-LeMonda (Eds.), *Child psychology: A handbook of contemporary issues* (pp. 145–171). Philadelphia, PA: Psychology Press.

A Work from a Literary Anthology or an Edition Other than the First

The work drawn from a larger text must be listed first, then the title of the book itself is given. When there are a large number of editors (eight in this case), list only the lead editor followed by "et al." (which means "and others"). The fact that this is a second edition is noted after the title of the complete text.

> Shakespeare, W. (1997). *Othello*. In G. B. Evans et al. (Eds.), *The Riverside Shakespeare* (2nd ed., pp. 1251–1288). New York, NY: Houghton Mifflin.

Two (or More) Books by the Same Author or a Revised Edition

Books with the same author are listed in order of publication, the earliest date listed first. If the dates are the same, use the works' titles to list them alphabetically (excluding articles such as "A," "An," and "The"). If you have two or more authors with the same last name, arrange them alphabetically by the initials of their first names.

> McBrien, R. P. (1994). *Catholicism* (Rev. ed.). New York, NY: HarperCollins.
> McBrien, R. P. (1996). *Responses to 101 questions on the Church*. New York, NY: Paulist Press.

Book with a Title Within a Title

Distinguish a title, such as that of Sylvia Plath's novel *The Bell Jar,* within the title of another work by italicizing only the novel's title, not the complete title of the work you are citing:

Macpherson, P. (1991). Reflecting on *The bell jar.* New York, NY: Routledge.

Book or Brochure with a Corporate Author

In the case of corporate authorship, the group or entity (often a governmental agency) is treated as the author and is alphabetized by the first significant word in its name. If the document is a brochure, identify it as such in brackets directly after the title: "[Brochure]."

American Heart Association. (1998). *Living well, staying well: The ultimate guide to help prevent heart disease and cancer* [Brochure]. New York, NY: Clarkson Potter.

Book with an Unknown (Anonymous) Author

An anonymous work is listed in the references section of your paper by the first significant word in the title, in this instance, alphabetically under "M." Note that this text is translated and was originally published in the 10th century.

The Mabinogion. (J. Gantz, Trans.) (1976). New York, NY: Penguin. (Original work published 10th century)

Graphic Novels and Comics

Graphic narratives are sometimes the work of several people and sometimes the product of a single author and illustrator. Treat a single-author entry like you would any other single-author book entry (as in the Smith example below), but list the roles of other contributors to a collaborative work.

Moore, A. (Writer), Gibbons, D. (Illustrator), & Mark, B. (Ed.). (1995). *Watchmen.* New York, NY: DC Comics.

Sacred Texts

While the APA style does not specifically require documentation for sacred texts beyond the level of in-text citations, some professors do because of the range of translations now available: don't forget to include both the particular edition and the editor(s) in your citation.

Coogan, M. D., et al. (Eds.). (2001). *The new Oxford annotated Bible: New revised standard version* (3rd ed.). New York, NY: Oxford University Press.

Tanakh: A new translation of the holy scriptures according to the traditional Hebrew text. (1985). Philadelphia, PA: Jewish Publication Society.

Books in More than One Volume

Behn, A. (1967). *Oroonoko.* In M. Summers (Ed.), *The works of Aphra Behn* (Vol. 5). New York, NY: Benjamin Blom. (Original work published 1688)

Dictionaries

As a general rule, the best advice for quoting general dictionaries of standard American English is don't. Unless the word is obscure or has changed in meaning over time (e.g., "pretend" can mean "to aspire to"), it is considered common knowledge and you do not need to cite it. Resist the urge to begin an essay by citing a dictionary definition (Please—trust us on this) unless the word is truly one your professor or target audience is unlikely to know—this may include arcane medical terminology, recent slang, specific legal terms, etc. *The Oxford English Dictionary,* widely considered the most authoritative dictionary, covers word usage over time. Use your desk dictionary often, but cite it sparingly. Most professors will be impressed, not annoyed, if you accurately use a current English word that they need to look up. The exception to this general rule is when you employ a special-area dictionary, such as a dictionary of medical or legal terms.

> Langmuir, E., & Lynton, N. (Eds.). (2000). *The Yale dictionary of art and artists.* New Haven, CT: Yale University Press.

Encyclopedias

As with dictionaries, encyclopedia entries are generally arranged alphabetically, but unlike dictionaries, you must indicate both volume and page numbers when citing encyclopedias. If the entry has a named author, list that author's name first, as you would with any other source. Note that the abbreviation for "Editor" is capitalized while the abbreviation for "edition" is not. If you are using a common reference book with a large number of editors—such as *The Encyclopaedia Britannica* or *The Encyclopedia Americana*—you may list only the lead editor, followed by "et al." (meaning "and others"):

> Corsini, R. J., et al. (Eds.). (1994). *Encyclopedia of psychology* (2nd ed., Vol. 3, pp. 15–21). New York, NY: Wiley.

Other Print Sources

Government Publications

When citing government publications, treat the specific governmental (federal, state, county, city) agency as the author. Government publications often require more patience and fortitude to research because of their great volume. Many federal government publications come from the Government Printing Office (GPO) in Washington, DC, which publishes bills, resolutions, reports, and miscellaneous documents from the House and Senate. Here are common abbreviations you may run into when researching GPO documents: Congressional Record—Cong. Rec.; House of Representatives—H or HR; Senate—S or Sen.; resolution—Res.; document—Doc.; and department—Dept.

U.S. Department of Health and Human Services. (1988). *The Surgeon General's report on nutrition and health.* Washington, DC: Government Printing Office.

Dissertation or Abstract

Pringle, M. W. (2000). Seizing the moral high ground: The discourses of alcohol in American literature. *Dissertation Abstracts International: 61,* 10A.

Published Proceedings of a Conference

Tammany, J. E. (1984). Peer Gynt: In the desert. In D. Konstan & C. Shabrawy (Eds.), *Proceedings of the International Conference in Comparative Drama* (pp. 67–82). Cairo, Egypt: American University in Cairo Press.

Legal Documents

Legal citations are full of obscure abbreviations and can be difficult to cite fully and correctly. The requirements for citing such sources is beyond the scope of this book except in their most basic forms. *The Bluebook: A Uniform System of Citation* is the definitive source for the citation of legal documents. You can refer to famous court cases such as *Roe v. Wade* or *Brown v. Board of Education* simply by name. Here is a basic citation:

Court Ruling

Zacchini v. Scripps-Howard Broadcasting Company, 433 U.S. 562, 97 S. Ct. 2849 (1977).

Exceptions to the Rule: Personal Communications, Maps, and Charts

While APA style requires that you provide an in-text citation for personal interviews, telephone conversations, e-mail letters and postcards. They are not considered "recoverable data" because they are not archived, and therefore are not listed in the references section.

Maps and charts should be cited in a footnote on the same page on which they appear (see the example on page 31) rather than on the references page.

Unpublished Manuscripts and Typescripts

When citing an unpublished handwritten manuscript or typescript, list the title of the collection (if it has one) and its location.

Hopkins, G. M. (n.d.). *Gerard Manley Hopkins manuscript collection.* Unpublished manuscript, Gonzaga University in Spokane, WA.

Nonprint Sources

Television Broadcast

List the producer, the date the program aired, and its title. Use "[Television broadcast]" to denote medium, and put other descriptive data in the brackets as well. End with the city of the show's origin, and the network/service.

> Crystal, L. (Executive Producer). (2005, June 27). Interview with J. C. Greenburg. *The news hour with Jim Lehrer* [Television broadcast, New York, NY: Public Broadcasting Service.

Motion Picture

Begin with the producer(s), director, and writer if that information is available, then list the title followed by the descriptor "[Motion picture]," and finish with the country of origin and studio.

> Baussy, D. (Producer & Director), & Januszczak, W. (Writer). (1985). *Picasso: Portrait of an artist* [Motion picture]. France: RM Arts.

> Bender, L. (Producer), & Tarantino, Q. (Writer & Director). (1994). *Pulp fiction* [Motion picture]. United States: Miramax Films.

Music Recording

Give the writer, copyright date, title of the song, recording artist if other than the writer, title of the album, followed by the medium [Record], place, and label.

> Wonder, S. (1995). Master blaster. On *Natural wonder* [CD]. Los Angeles, CA: Motown Records.

Winging It: How to Cite Unusual Sources

If it has useful information, it can be a valid research resource, and it can be cited. If you come across an unusual source for which you cannot find a model, you can still effectively cite it. Keep in mind the basic formula—Author. (Date). *Title*. Place of Publication: Publisher—and make a list of the information available from your source. Be sure to assign it a working title when none is established (Statue, Tin, Cartoon, etc.). For example, the Republic of Tea Company prints a chart of the caffeine content (per 5-ounce measure) of coffee, black tea, oolong tea, and green tea on its tea tins. In an essay on the coffee culture in America, such a source could prove useful even if there is no model to follow. Below are examples of how we would improvise unusual references.

> Bernini, G. (n.d.). *Rape of Proserpine* [Marble Statue]. Museo e Galleria Borghese, Rome, Italy.

> Caffeine content. (2004). [Tea Tin]. Novato, CA: The Republic of Tea Co.

> Duncan, A. (1988). *Enigma: A game of riddles* [Board Game]. Edinburgh, Scotland Drumond Park.

Important safeguards. (2001). *Eureka lightweight upright vacuum cleaner owner's manual* (p. 2). Bloomington, IN: Eureka.

Wilson, G. (2005, June 27). [Cartoon]. *New Yorker,* p. 65.

Be creative and resourceful. Who knows what useful and pertinent sources you may find beyond these hypothetical possibilities!

Credits

Index